ROUTLEDGE LIBRARY EDITIONS:
LIBRARY AND INFORMATION SCIENCE

Volume 53

LIBRARY NETWORKING:
CURRENT PROBLEMS AND
FUTURE PROSPECTS

LIBRARY NETWORKING: CURRENT PROBLEMS AND FUTURE PROSPECTS

Papers Based on the Symposium "Networking: Where from Here?"

Edited by
WILSON LUQUIRE

LONDON AND NEW YORK

First published in 1983 by The Haworth Press, Inc.

This edition first published in 2020
by Routledge
2 Park Square, Milton Park, Abingdon, Oxon OX14 4RN

and by Routledge
52 Vanderbilt Avenue, New York, NY 10017

Routledge is an imprint of the Taylor & Francis Group, an informa business

© 1983 The Haworth Press, Inc.

All rights reserved. No part of this book may be reprinted or reproduced or utilised in any form or by any electronic, mechanical, or other means, now known or hereafter invented, including photocopying and recording, or in any information storage or retrieval system, without permission in writing from the publishers.

Trademark notice: Product or corporate names may be trademarks or registered trademarks, and are used only for identification and explanation without intent to infringe.

British Library Cataloguing in Publication Data
A catalogue record for this book is available from the British Library

ISBN: 978-0-367-34616-4 (Set)
ISBN: 978-0-429-34352-0 (Set) (ebk)
ISBN: 978-0-367-40371-3 (Volume 53) (hbk)
ISBN: 978-0-367-40378-2 (Volume 53) (pbk)
ISBN: 978-0-429-35572-1 (Volume 53) (ebk)

Publisher's Note
The publisher has gone to great lengths to ensure the quality of this reprint but points out that some imperfections in the original copies may be apparent.

Disclaimer
The publisher has made every effort to trace copyright holders and would welcome correspondence from those they have been unable to trace.

Library Networking: Current Problems and Future Prospects

Papers Based on the Symposium
"Networking: Where from Here?"

Wilson Luquire
Editor

The Haworth Press
New York

Library Networking: Current Problems and Future Prospects has also been published as *Resource Sharing & Information Networks,* Volume 1, Numbers 1/2, Fall/Winter 1983.

Copyright © 1983 by The Haworth Press, Inc. All rights reserved. Copies of articles in this publication may be reproduced noncommercially for the purpose of educational advancement. Otherwise, no part of this work may be reproduced or utilized in any form or by any means, electronic or mechanical including photocopying, microfilm, and recording, or by any information storage and retrieval system without permission in writing from the publisher. Printed in the United States of America.

The Haworth Press, Inc., 28 East 22 Street, New York, NY 10010

Library of Congress Cataloging in Publication Data
Main entry under title:

Library networking—current problems and future prospects.

"Has also been published as Resource sharing & information networks, volume 1, numbers 1/2, fall/winter 1983"—T.P. verso.
Includes bibliographical references.
1. Library information networks—United States—Congresses. 2. Library cooperation—United States—Congresses. I. Luquire, Wilson.
Z674.8.L49   1983   021.6'5   83-18474
ISBN 0-86656-270-2

Library Networking: Current Problems and Future Prospects

Papers Based on the Symposium
"Networking: Where from Here?"

Resource Sharing & Information Networks
Volume 1, Numbers 1/2

CONTENTS

FROM THE EDITOR	1
Welcome	3
David Kaser, Professor, School of Library and Information Science, Indiana University, Bloomington, Indiana	
The Honorable Jim Edgar, *Secretary of State and State Librarian, Springfield, Illinois*	5
Barbara Markuson, *Executive Director, INCOLSA, Indianapolis, Indiana*	19
Frank P. Grisham, *Executive Director, SOLINET, Atlanta, Georgia*	33
Laima Mockus, *Executive Director, NELINET, Newton, Massachusetts*	45
Introduction for Afternoon Session	57
David Kaser, Moderator	
Richard McCoy, *President, RLG, Inc., Stanford, California*	59

Rowland Brown, *President and Chief Executive Officer,
OCLC, Inc., Dublin, Ohio*   73

Toni Carbo Bearman, *Executive Director, National
Commission on Libraries and Information Science,
Washington, DC*   87

Panel Discussion   99
           David Kaser, Moderator

FROM THE EDITOR

This issue is dedicated to the proceedings of the April 12, 1983 symposium "Networking: Where From Here?" held in Champaign, Illinois. The speakers represented state, regional, and national networks and the National Commission on Libraries and Information Science.

The journal is an exact recap, inasmuch as possible, of the day's activities. There was a clear understanding with the seven speakers and moderator that no formally submitted papers were being requested. An attempt has been made to have you relive the symposium as it occurred on April 12th. The panel discussion has also been recounted similarly.

The speakers' remarks were directed toward "Networking: Where From Here?" in relationship to their specific affiliation with state, regional, or national networks.

Wilson Luquire
Editor

Welcome

David Kaser

Professor, School of Library and Information Science
Indiana University
Bloomington, Indiana

My name is David Kaser and I'm your interlocutor here today. This means that this is a somewhat honorific, but not particularly onerous assignment that I have here. I will contribute nothing substantive to the day's activities, but we do have plenty of good speakers to do that for us.

Before we begin the program today, I'd like to invite your attention to a couple of announcements. You'll notice you're wearing a white name tag. If you need help in anything, they tell me there are people walking around with blue name tags who are members of the staff and who will be glad to help you in any way they can. They also tell me that the speakers are supposed to be wearing yellow name tags—and I'm not sure how I feel about that. I notice that our first speaker hasn't even put his on, and I don't blame him in that regard.

As we proceed through the morning and also the afternoon, we will not have questions until the end of all presentations. As you develop questions in your thinking during the course of these presentations, if you would please, make notes of them. You'll notice in the program we will convene in a panel format. At that time, the major work will revolve around the questions that we anticipate you will have by that time. So please, do make notes of the questions that you have. There will be, also, no real breaks between now and noon. At that time, of course, we'll break for lunch and then, from 1:30 until 3:00, there will also be no breaks.

You might be interested in knowing that we have 265 registered in attendance here today which, I think, is quite good. There are people from as far away as both coasts, and from two other countries who came. I think one, the most distant, came from Taiwan to be with us for this conference here today. There are, of course, many distinguished guests in the audience—too many for us to introduce. I'm sure we'd have 265 introductions if you were to attempt to do that.

The Honorable Jim Edgar

Secretary of State and State Librarian
Springfield, Illinois

(Introductory Remarks by David Kaser)

It was my pleasure (a year or two ago) to be seated one evening at dinner down at Eastern Illinois University next to our first speaker. I think it says something about his political acumen that, at the end of dinner, he knew everything there was to know about me; and I knew nothing at all about him. But he is a delightful dinner table conversationalist as, I'm sure, you would understand under those circumstances.

He has, as we know, been a very successful politician beginning, I think when he was a child; certainly, when he was a student at Eastern when he served as Student Body President. At age thirty, he came into the Illinois House and has now, for the last several years, been the Secretary of State—of this State.

It is my pleasure to introduce to you at this time, the Honorable Jim Edgar.

* * *

I'm delighted to be here. When I first was asked to speak, they said that Eastern was going to sponsor this Symposium and I couldn't figure out why we were doing it in Champaign. When I got here and I saw that, of course, the University of Illinois was involved, too, I understood.

As one who grew up in Charleston and went to Eastern, I was always used to the shadow of the big University up north and I have had some good go-arounds with the State Legislators from the Champaign District. But I think cooperation is typical, though, of what I have found in the library community. In the political arena or even in the academic world we might compete between regions, but

6   *Library Networking: Current Problems and Future Prospects*

JIM EDGAR: "Cooperation is the strength of the library community in this State . . . Sharing resources to fill users' needs is the cornerstone of a special partnership here in Illinois."

in the library community there seems to be a genuine sense of cooperation and working together, and I think that is what this Conference is all about. What I have found in my two years now as Secretary of State, and more importantly, as State Librarian, is that cooperation is the strength of the library community in this State, and, I think, throughout the Nation. There are many of you from out of the State, but those of us in Illinois are especially proud of our efforts here.

I would, also, as a state official, like to welcome those of you from out of the State of Illinois. I'm especially impressed that people came from as far away as Taiwan. A couple of years ago I made that trip and it is a long way to go to a meeting, but we're delighted to have you here. We're more delighted to have your money here and hope that you spend it all while you're in Illinois. We need it. And I'm sure the Champaign-Urbana Chamber of Commerce hopes all the rest of you from Illinois spend your money while you're here, too. I am sorry that I won't be able to be here all day. Maybe it's a good thing. I can speak and leave. But it sounds like it will be an extremely interesting Conference and, again, I'm privileged and honored to be asked to take part in it.

"Networking," before I became Secretary of State and State Librarian, I didn't really know what it was all about. I lived in Charleston. I was a State Legislator. I knew Lincoln Trail existed because that was the only way I could get certain films about state government from my public library. But, I don't think the average person in this State, or in the Nation, probably appreciates all the things that go on in the library community, the networks that are set up, and the sharing that goes on. As I said earlier, I think that this cooperation is one of the strengths of the library community, and I think it is important that the library community make the public aware of networks and the services they offer. Sharing resources to fill users needs is the cornerstone of a special partnership here in Illinois. This resource partnership is called the Illinois Library and Information Network (ILLINET). ILLINET was created in 1965 as a public library network. It was not organized as a computer based network. It is a multi-layered, multi-purpose, multi-type library cooperative. ILLINET is the combined human and material resources of over 2,000 public, special, academic, and school libraries. In ILLINET, the human resources are the most important. We are the ones who must insure that the library resources of the networks are available for the users.

The people of ILLINET face two great challenges through the beginning of the 21st century; the effective use of developing technology, and anticipating the changing needs of the people we are committed to serve. These are the issues I wish to address today. It seems now that the benefits of technology are being shouted from every home and library rooftop in the land. It was not very long ago that there were very few who perceived the importance of computers for libraries. One of the first was the On-line Computer Library Center, OCLC. Illinois responded to their leadership by establishing the ILLINET Bibliographic Data Base Service, which serves Illinois libraries by providing several automated library activities through OCLC. The total administration and organization of the program has been incorporated into the State Library annual budget. The State Library through its contact with OCLC manages the network of Illinois libraries participating in the service. Each participating library contracts with the State Library for training, liaison, payment, and other network services. We pass on to the user institutions only direct costs for OCLC. No operational or administrative costs are passed on. Because of the resource sharing potential of OCLC, interest remains extremely high and ILLINET participation is expected to grow. Initiated in the mid '70s, the ILLINET Bibliographic Data Base Service serves over two hundred thirty libraries of all types. While OCLC services are fundamental in building a firm foundation for improvement of library service with ILLINET, they are only one of the many databased uses of technology funded by ILLINET. For the last two years, the State Library has encouraged the sharing of automated circulations systems to serve all types of libraries and to provide on-line catalogs for regional library sharing. The configuration of these automated systems varies. In some cases a single computer system is utilized. In other cases, a single computer system is being shared by as many as thirty libraries in neighboring communities. A variety of automated systems is used, including Data Phase, Computer Library Systems Incorporated and Data Research Associates. The electronic systems allow ILLINET members to use each other's resources by identifying where the material is located, and indicating if the item is on the shelf and available for loan. Using circulation systems as resource sharing tools has been most successful with several regional cooperatives using the same equipment and searching each other's computers.

Because of the variety of technology currently available and to insure users a standard means of access to the broad spectrum of bibliographic and information data, the Illinois State Library created the Advisory Automation Committee to help devise a method of interfacing the different computer systems. The committee is made up of representatives of the public and private sectors, as well as the Illinois library community. The Advisory Automation Committee has been assigned three charges: 1) assisting in the solution of specific library automation problems, such as interfacing existing systems, 2) devising a means to encourage standardization of protocol and database construction whenever possible, and 3) recommending strategies for future ILLINET automation projects and programs. Solving the problems presented by technology in ILLINET will keep the human element of ILLINET busy for years to come. The work of the Advisory Automation Committee and others sensitive to the impact of technology in libraries will enhance resource sharing and multi-type aspects of library and information services in Illinois.

Another creative approach, that Illinois has taken to library networking is our cooperation with the Library Computer System, LCS. LCS connects thirteen academic libraries, including the University of Illinois, providing statewide access to over twenty million volumes. Eighteen regional library cooperatives have been given LCS terminals to search the collections of the LCS Libraries in the computer system. Once an item is found, it can be ordered by simply typing a request on the terminal. The use of circulation systems to request interlibrary loan materials is providing Illinois citizens with decreased turn around time for receipt of materials and an increased number of available titles with few bureaucratic or procedural problems. Locating the material needed for an interlibrary loan has been made easy and relatively inexpensive using OCLC and other automated circulation systems. However, it is only the first step toward getting the materials to the patrons. Once the book is found and we know that it is available for loan, it is most important not to lose time in transit. ILLINET has solved the problem of slow and undependable postal service—I hope there's no one from the postal service here. I kind of hate to attack other governmental agencies—by using LSCA funding to administer the Illinois Library Delivery Service. This year for the first time I've included partial state funding in the State Library budget for this essential compo-

JIM EDGAR: "Having access to library materials through technology does little good unless ILLINET can guarantee that the books people need are being purchased, which brings us to the second challenge facing ILLINET in the coming years. Shared data bases will prevent needless duplication and promote prompt delivery of materials. However, it is through cooperative collection development that we can find the best methods of addressing the challenge of sharing in a reasonable, rational, and cost effective manner."

nent of ILLINET. This service provides daily van service between libraries in all areas of the State. Library material can now be delivered from anywhere in the State within twenty-four hours.

I have just described to you some of the ways ILLINET has met the challenge of using computers to meet the needs of library users. But what about anticipating the changing needs of library users? Having access to library materials through technology does little good unless ILLINET can guarantee that the books people need are being purchased, which brings us to the second challenge facing IL-LINET in the coming years. Shared databases will prevent needless duplication and promote prompt delivery of materials. However, it is through cooperative collection development that we can find the best method of addressing the challenge of sharing in a reasonable, rational, and cost effective manner. The Illinois State Library is committed to cooperative collection development and to the interdependency inherent in network resource building. Effective collection development must be based upon systematic network-wide analysis. Currently in Illinois, there are a number of collection development projects underway addressing the issue at regional and local levels. One approach to resource sharing is being examined in an LSCA funded project entitled, "Implementation of Coordinated Cooperative Collection Development, a Planning Model for Systems." Library people sure like long titles, I must say. I understand now why you use so many initials. I was giving a speech on this once, and they thought I was a New Deal Democrat. Initiated in 1982, the purpose of the project is to develop a process for cooperative collection development among all types of libraries. Emphasis is being placed on developing user-oriented acquisition policies at the local level and determining subject collection responsibilities at the system level. When applied to ILLINET, the process should help identify responsibilities at the research and reference centers and other special resource centers. The basis of the process is a method developed by King Research to assess library collection strengths and weaknesses. This method was developed at the Illinois Valley Library System with LSCA Title III funds as an interlibrary cooperation project. We are looking forward to tangible results from the project which will include: collection development policies at the local level, a system cooperative collection development policy and a manual describing the step-by-step process of accomplishing these tasks. As a long-range result of the project, we expect increased interlibrary loan fill rates at the local and system level,

JIM EDGAR: "The ability for a user to walk into any size library and to have a larger world of information at his or her fingertip is something that must be guaranteed to all library patrons."

improved response time in interlibrary loan and back-up records, and more effective utilization of existing library collections and material budgets.

Also underway in the Illinois Valley Library System is an experimental resource sharing project. This LSCA funded project is being used to experiment with OCLC in testing some things that we think have importance to ILLINET. The cost effectiveness of the cataloging subsystem of OCLC is well documented in larger institutions. We felt a need to investigate to what extent OCLC can be cost effective for smaller units of library services. This project is an attempt to discover ways for libraries of various sizes and types, in cooperative systems like Illinois Valley, to use terminals not only for sharing cataloging data but also for sharing library materials, and to do so in a cost effective way to the benefit of users. Underlying all this is the need to discover if smaller units of library services can be effective contributors in a network resource sharing. The ability for a user to walk into any size library and to have a larger world of information at his or her fingertip is something that must be guaranteed to all library patrons. I think that is especially important to me, one who grew up in a smaller community, though Charleston with Eastern Illinois University had a lot of resources. But, I also spend a lot of time in smaller communities of Illinois, some towns not over 1,000. Making sure that no matter where they live in the state that people have access to the same services as those living in metropolitan areas is an extremely important goal, not only here in Illinois, but throughout the nation.

The Illinois Library Valley System is a prime innovator in cooperative collection development in Illinois. However, the Lincoln Trail Library System, one of our hosts here today, has developed another approach to cooperative collection development. By analyzing interlibrary loan requests from Lincoln Trail Libraries from January 1979 through March 1981, Lincoln Trail was able to identify not only what requests were being filled in the systems, but what requests were not being filled. As a result, the system established a program of matching grants to system members to encourage selective collection development. Materials acquired through the program are input in the Lincoln Trail database in order to guarantee access to all.

On-line catalogs, interlibrary loan and collection development are a few of the services available through ILLINET. Other programs developed by the network are ongoing, continuing education programs for library trustees and library friends. Funding of eighteen regional library systems has provided librarians with specialized consulting in areas of library administration and organization, AV collection, back-up reference centers and system-wide local delivery services. Services to the blind, the physically handicapped and to those confined to institutions have been made possible through ILLINET.

Now that we have addressed some of the challenges ILLINET has met, what does the future hold? We foresee that among the great challenges lying ahead for us in Illinois will be the challenge of telecommunications as it will affect libraries and resource sharing in the future. We will be seeking means to provide access and linkage for the various systems presently operational throughout Illinois, as well as determining the most economical means of providing these data communication links. Careful consideration will be given to determining modes of access based upon an analysis of levels of use. In the next several months, the Illinois State Library Advisory Automation Committee will be preparing a request for proposals to prepare the first stage of a long series of projects that will lead to an improved data communication network for all Illinois libraries. We expect to move ahead in these areas, with due consideration to similar application of telecommunication linkage being planned in library communites and other related institutions.

I mentioned earlier that ILLINET started as eighteen public library systems. More than ten years ago academic, school, and special libraries were invited to become affiliated or participating members in the systems and more than seventeen hundred of them have done so. These libraries bring resources and expertise of great value to all library users of Illinois and because of their participation in sharing should have a voice in the government of these systems. The library community in Illinois, after much deliberation, decided that, in those areas that were ready, full representation on the boards of the libraries should be made possible. The Illinois General Assembly is considering, this week in committee, legislation to authorize true multi-typing for those library systems that are ready to move in that direction. This is yet another important step in the process of assuring that all resources available in the State are shared and available to all our users.

During the past two years, we have been able to make significant improvements in the funding of our libraries and library systems in Illinois. We have been able to achieve this by convincing the legislature of the importance of supporting the services libraries provide. We have increased per capita grants to local libraries from .21ᶜ per capita in FY '81, when I took office, to just under .51ᶜ for FY '83. We have also achieved, in conjunction with the Illinois Library Association, a formula increase for the systems for the first time in four years. Shortly, I will be introducing my FY '84 budget in the Illinois General Assembly. I'm very pleased to tell you that I've been able to include a 5% increase for FY '83 appropriations for library grants. However, and this is an important, "however", in order for that increase to be approved, it is essential that the State receive additional revenue. Now that's the word that my staff used. Let me just put it to you very plainly. We're going to have to raise taxes, and that means the income tax, and that's what this session in the General Assembly is all about. Without more revenue, the increase I have requested for libraries will almost certainly be unattainable, and it's very possible that without a revenue increase in this State, you will actually see a cut below our current level of funding. So, I just can't stress enough how important I think it is to communicate your feelings to the members of the General Assembly on this very important issue, and I also think it is important to make the community aware of the services they may not have if such a revenue increase is not realized in this session of the General Assembly.

It is only by working together that we can continue to make strides. Now those of the rest of you from out of Illinois don't have to worry about this, you've got all kinds of money. I know those of you from Indiana have already raised your taxes and so have most other states. Our problem in Illinois is that we were a little better off in Illinois, so now we're a lot slower in reacting to the problems. But to those of you in Illinois, this message is for you. It's only by working together that we can continue to make strides in increasing funding for our libraries. As with so much of what we do, the ultimate approval must come from the legislature, whether it be at the Illinois General Assembly level or in the Federal Congress in Washington. As I have said on many occasions and in many places, I've been very impressed with the resources that the library community can bring to bear on the legislative process on issues with which they are concerned. It is very important for all of us, whether from public, special, academic, school or institution libraries, to be constantly involved in the legislative process, both on issues of program or policy funding. This is true, not only here in Illinois, but also on the national level. Illinois has been very lucky over the last several years to receive substantial amounts of LSCA funds, and those funds, because of the foresight of the Illinois State Library Advisory Committee, have been absolutely essential to the development and expansion of the network in Illinois. We have a responsibility to see that this continues. At the state level, the impact of our actions, or lack of action, will be even more immediately felt. Your ability to influence the legislative process in Springfield will determine the success of our efforts to increase funding and expand the services to the citizens of Illinois. It is my hope and, indeed, my request that all of you realize the importance of your involvement with the legislative process and its relationship to the future of networking here in Illinois and, I'm sure, throughout the nation.

Again, it's been my pleasure to be here this morning and to share a few thoughts with you. And as I said, I get the honor, I guess, and the advantage of talking and running. But, there are several people here from the State Library, if you have any complaints check with them. I'm sure that they can answer any questions or comments. Again, I'd like to welcome you to Illinois, those of you from out of state and all of you whether you're from Illinois or out of state. I've enjoyed very much the past two years as State Librarian and working with you in the spirit of cooperation that I find at all the library meetings that I attend. This spirit of cooperation is extremely important, and it is very important, I think, that we get out to the public, particularly the public that is sitting right now in Springfield and in Congress in Washington. Librarians, I have said many times, stretch the public dollar farther than any other public body I know, and, I think, networking is a good example of how you stretch that dollar. We're going to have to continue to stretch dollars, and if we don't do our job talking to our elective representatives, we're going to have fewer dollars to stretch. Again, I'm delighted to be here. Hope you have a successful Conference. Thank you very much.

* * *

David Kaser

Thank you very much, Jim. We're grateful to you for this inspiring opening to this conference.

I'm sure that all of us here understand why you have to leave. He has a helicopter parked outdoors and tells me that he has to get back to Chicago right away. I immediately, of course thought of the elec-

JIM EDGAR: "Librarians, I have said many times, stretch the public dollar farther than any other public body I know, and, I think, networking is a good example of how you stretch that dollar."

tion; but he says "no." He has to go to a White Sox opener this afternoon. He did say that following the game, he plans to go to a victory banquet—he didn't say who he thought was going to win.

At any rate, we're grateful to you for being with us on this, I'm sure, busy day for you in your office.

Barbara Markuson

Executive Director, INCOLSA
Indianapolis, Indiana

(Introductory Remarks by David Kaser)

James Whitcomb Riley once said that you should never ask a person if he's a Hoosier; because if he is he will tell you, and if he isn't you will just make him feel bad. Well, our next speaker is (as I am) a Hoosier—at least has been for the last eight years.

I don't know what we ever did to deserve her in her present role as Executive Director of INCOLSA (which is our initialism for Indiana Cooperative Library Services Authority), because our speaker has been in the vanguard of library networking and automation for a long, long time; much longer than her youthful appearance would indicate to you.

I remember I first became acquainted with her, twenty years ago next month, at one of the most exciting conferences I've ever had the pleasure of attending. The National Science Foundation and the Council on Library Resources convoked a group of—I don't remember how many—sixty or eighty librarians and computer people who had, up to that time, not said a civil word to one another; and made us stay for four or five days—perhaps Barbara will remember how long it was—at a think tank in Northern Virginia, just to get acquainted with one another. By the end of the week, we librarians were occasionally, with much diffidence and not any confidence at all, attempting to use a computer term. The computer people were (with equal diffidence) occasionally trying to use a library term. That was the beginning of a dialogue; the beginning of a very useful dialogue.

Barbara was there, presenting a portion of the Library of Congress' presentation at that time. As I said, she's been in the leadership of this movement ever since.

It is my pleasure at this time to introduce to you a fellow Hoosier—Barbara Markuson.

* * *

At the Arlie House Conference on Interlibrary Cooperation and Information Networks, held in 1970, attendees, for the most part, fell into one of two camps. There were those who believed that a national network would be planned at the national level and those who believed that it would evolve from independent grass roots efforts. That the former group held all the aces is evidenced by a resolution passed at the Conference asking that the National Commission on Libraries and Information Science (NCLIS):

1. Design a comprehensive plan to facilitate cooperative development of the nation's libraries, information centers and other knowledge resources, and
2. To coordinate development of the nation's plans for a library and information network.

The scene described above is typical of many past and present national network meetings. Usually there is an effort to coalesce opinion on very broad issues. Then there is usually some attempt at group action to move things forward by passing resolutions, appointing study committees, or taking some other general approach. Although one may have been present and caught up in the spirit of such gatherings, one is often struck later with the fact that only a passing nod was given to organization, funding, technical requirements, and the many other details essential to implementation.

One result of this approach is that expectations may be raised when, in fact, it may take decades to achieve national goals, if at all. On the other hand, this kind of group consensus assures that we begin planning at a very high level of abstraction so that we can concentrate on very broad issues and principles. Clearly, if we got down to specifics too soon, the group would begin to fragment immediately. Thus, we can begin quite early in a new technical milieu to conceptualize general goals, develop a professional awareness of the new technology, and begin to build broad support, even though we may be quite ignorant about the changes required to apply the technology and what it would take to implement a new design for library and information service.

Tanenbaum, in his book, *Computer Networks,* considers the peer process of abstraction to be crucial to all network design. Before we can develop a network, we must first go through the abstract process of conceptualizing what the network will do, how it should operate, how it will be organized, and so on. This process must be shared by enough people to generate the critical mass necessary to get the network underway. This process is fundamental to implementation, Tanenbaum believes, for without it, it is impossible to partition the design of the complete network, which is, in fact, an unmanageable design problem, into several smaller and more manageable, problems.

For the past two decades, through meetings, papers, and studies, the concept of a national network comprised of linking regional and state networks has served as our broadest conceptual model. It has been tacitly assumed that each state would have some type of network that would, in turn, link individual libraries into area networks. It was also assumed that state networks would benefit from, and not duplicate, national standards, a national telecommunications network, national level services, such as MARC, and national-level coordination and funding.

As we begin the third decade of network development, there is still a strong belief in the integral role of the state in networking. We will examine briefly whether our abstract models of networking are changing and, if so, how. The views expressed here are those of the author and are not official views of the Indiana Cooperative Library Services Authority.

THE NETWORK ENTREPRENEURS

Although there has been a lot of discussion about a national network effort, there has been no serious attempt to build one. That is, no single agency or group of agencies actually developed plans and sought funding for implementation. Therefore, as ideas about possible network services and functions began to take hold, any enterprising individual or group could seek funding, through development grants, the budget process, or from commercial sources to build components of the network.

The delivery of information retrieval services has largely been provided by commercial enterprises. Provision of bibliographic database records has largely been a service of the national libraries.

Development of stand alone local or area turnkey networks to support one or more library functions has until very recently been the province of the commercial vendor. Resource sharing and interlibrary loan have been promoted at the state level by state library agencies working through consortia of various types, and at the national level by specialized agencies such as the National Library of Medicine. The development of large-scale technical processing and cataloging support databases has been the speciality of cooperative state and regional networks and the non-profit bibliographic utilities.

The evolution toward an automated library and information network has, perhaps, been far more complex and diffuse than was foreseen. Certainly, the neat hierarchical organization charts linking the various levels from the local library to national and international agencies only fit portions of the network. In the evolutionary process, certain organisms—so to speak—found that if they could adapt rapidly enough, there were niches that they could occupy and exploit. Early planners perhaps did not give enough attention to the tremendous specialization, need for capital, and competition that would result, given the lack of a viable, well-funded structure for library networking.

That networking could not be accommodated within the existing library structure can be illustrated by the number of organizations that have been created within the past two decades. Among these are: BRS, CLSI, Dataphase, OCLC, WLN, RLG, SOLINET, AMIGOS, MINNITEX, and INCOLSA. This extraordinary increase in extra-library organizations was a response to a need for risk-taking, capital, long-term development, cost-sharing, technical manpower, and large-scale technology transfer. It would be difficult for traditional library organizations to satisfy these needs.

However, individual libraries played an important role in network development. An obvious contribution is as user, and hence, financial supporter of network services. A less obvious role is that of experimenter and developer. Many present network services were first developed locally, and then were transferred to the field through more specialized organizations. Online catalogs and microcomputer applications are two recent examples of applications where more work is currently being done by libraries and library systems than by networks.

As we begin the third decade of networking, it seems likely that the number of network support organizations will increase. For example, organizations may form in response to new technologies such as electronic transmission of text. Other groups could integrate existing technologies in a new way, for example, a national library telecommunications system integrating satellite and other transmission technology could become a service of a new organization.

THE STATE NETWORK

In conceptualizing state network development, several scenarios were presented. In one scenario, the state network was the final link between the national hierarchical organization and the local library. It was to work through the hierarchy for resource sharing. Another scenario cast the state network in a central role as system designer and developer. This seemed reasonable considering that online network systems were then being developed by the Washington State Library and by a state network in Ohio called OCLC. A national system based on linked state network utilities was considered by many as the most logical evolution of a national network.

In fact, neither of these scenarios has yet come to pass. The first played out early when the impetus for national network development and implementation began to subside. The second lost momentum for reasons that are less clear but, perhaps, primarily because the needed risk capital was not available at the right time. Today only a few states are able to sustain network design and development efforts. Notable exceptions are the continued work on the Washington Library Network and the online catalog networks being developed by the University of Minnesota State University System and the University of California System.

If state networks have not formed the technical basis for networking, why is there such continued interest in them? One reason may be that state networks provide a structure through which we can bring certain aspects of networking down to a smaller, and perhaps more manageable, scale. A national document delivery system may be too difficult to implement, but several fine statewide systems are operational. The sheer mechanics of the national Union List of Serials lead to its demise, but many state union lists are flourishing. Reciprocal borrowing would be difficult to implement on a large scale, yet many states have introduced this service and (in Indiana at least) the volume of business is considerably larger than for interlibrary loan. A strong case can be made that state networks not only

BARBARA MARKUSON: "The issue of control is being raised more frequently. Exactly what 'control' means is never clearly expressed, but presumably there is only so much of it, so that if networks have more, libraries have less. It may well be that 'control' is a metaphor expressing uncertainty about the future."

complement national developments but, through these additional services, add value to them.

Although the euphoria about increased funding for libraries has subsided considerably since the White House Conference, a state network provides another approach for funding. Private non-profit networks have been active solicitors of private grants; public networks have the added potential of increasing the state funding for library services.

State networks also allow a broader participation than would be possible if the network were only at the regional or national level. A large resource of talented people can be tapped. Many contributions result from these efforts.

Of most significance however, is the role state networks play in transmitting new technology and concepts to the field. Through consulting, on-site training, workshops, demonstration projects, and contractual services, literally hundreds of libraries can be reached in a relatively short time. Through state networks these programs are usually available at a reasonable cost both in time and money. IN-COLSA, for example, has provided training in cataloging, MARC formats, operation of the OCLC system, microcomputers, automated circulation, information retrieval management, and specialized courses in various databases. Through demonstration projects, joint contracts for service, and other cooperative arrangement, many libraries are able to learn about and to participate in automated services that would not be feasible on an individual library basis.

NETWORKING: DECADE THREE

Despite the impressive contributions of computer-based networks, past success is no guarantee of a secure future. Indeed, to some, the very success of networks is cause for some concern. The issue of control is being raised more frequently. Exactly what "control" means is never clearly expressed, but presumably there is only so much of it, so that if networks have more, libraries have less. It may well be that "control" is a metaphor expressing uncertainty about the future: in the good old days, we all had control, so any technology that gives us control again is for the best.

Sara Fine also pointed out in a recent talk that people who are resistant to technological change often express this anxiety in terms of speed. "It's all moving so fast." "Things are changing too much and too quickly." "I can't keep up."

BARBARA MARKUSON: "The rapid proliferation of information technology is accelerating: videodisc, voice recognition, microcomputers, electronic printing, local area networking, etc. Each of these developments could make a profound change on libraries and library networks. Yet few of us have had time to study how these technologies will affect what we do."

Sometimes those who embrace technology feel the same way. The rapid proliferation of information technology is accelerating: videodisc, voice recognition, microcomputers, electronic printing, local area networking, etc. Each of these developments could make a profound change on libraries and library networks. Yet few of us have had time to study how these technologies will affect what we do. There are so many options that didn't exist ten years ago; many more scenarios—some threatening, some challenging.

Among many potential issues, I have identified six which are of special concern to state library networks. They are: decentralization, standards, linking, technical obsolesence, security, and appropriate technology for small libraries.

Decentralization: We need to understand that much of the discussion about decentralized networking is misleading. In a literal sense, "decentralized" means to redesign a centralized function so that it now operates from many points. However, many of the functions proposed for "decentralization" in library automation have been centralized in the first place. Examples include: online catalog access, automated circulation, and electronic printing. The point is a fine one, but it is important that we do not assume that we understand how all of these functions will fit together, how they will be kept in synch with higher level systems, and how one moves from one system to another.

Standards: With the exception of cataloging, there are virtually no standards for library technical development. Furthermore, the support for and promotion of development of standards continues at a wretched level. The prospect of efficient linkage, from both a technical and service aspect, will increasingly require that standards be developed and adopted within a reasonable time. As local area networking increases, the users will begin to question our solutions. Why should they have to cope with the variant display formats, search commands, loan periods, terminology, etc?

Linkage: The prospects for linkage of various computer systems into a functioning network seem no closer to fruition. The groups that will benefit most from these linkages are libraries and library users; yet most of the effort is being directed at the bibliographic utility level network. Until significant numbers of libraries and library networks refuse to buy systems unless they can provide standard linkages, it is unlikely that rapid progress can be made. The rapid proliferation of terminals and other equipment that can only be used for one application will continue unless we can get more

BARBARA MARKUSON: "However, many of the functions proposed for 'decentralization' in library automation have never been centralized in the first place."

user representation and more user input into decisions on linkage.

Technical Obsolescence: With online technology the library becomes dependent upon system components manufactured largely for business and industry. Competition demands that these represent the current deliverable state of the art: an equipment generation is now typically five years at most. After that, vendor support for system enhancement and for equipment maintenance will degrade, since the vendor's resources will bring more return if invested in newer technology.

Little attention has been given to how well typical library funding for equipment replacement, conversion, and retraining meshes with this fast cycle. Users of systems such as OCLC may not realize how many upgrades of hardware and software have occurred since they joined the system. OCLC and other networks have been able to keep equipment reasonably current by building replacement into the fee structure.

Library networks should help their members plan for budgeting techniques so that system replacement funds are accruing as the system becomes obsolete. The prospect of closing down an online catalog while voters review a bond issue or the legislature deliberates the needs for an increase in the library budget is not a happy one.

Security: A greater awareness of the need for increased security for computer systems that provide vital services to libraries is urgent. Disaster planning, backup systems, and security procedures are considerations that will become increasingly important as network systems get larger, as more library functions are online, and as smaller networks with fewer resources for security proliferate. Standards and guidelines, and educational programs would be a start.

Appropriate Technology for Small Libraries: There are two major aspects to this issue. First, there is the small library that needs technology at a low cost. Second, there is the specialized library with a small staff that has to handle many functions. In both instances, current technologies are often inappropriate due to the cost, the training required to achieve proficiency and the training required to keep abreast of enhancements. Very low cost equipment is now available that could be incorporated into many network systems. The need to provide low cost access for users of small libraries to state databases and area online catalogs is also a concern if we plan to achieve some reasonable equity of access. State networks can assist by funding

BARBARA MARKUSON: "First there is the small library that needs technology at a low cost. Second there is the specialized library with a small staff that has to handle many functions. In both instances, current technologies are often inappropriate due to the cost, the training required to achieve proficiency and to keep abreast of enhancements."

projects for appropriate technology and exploring options that provide some level of access for all types and sizes of libraries.

CONCLUSION

The technology of networking, the structure of networking, and the use of networks will be changing rapidly as more information technology is accommodated. State networks need to be flexible in service and funding arrangements to accommodate to contracting with different vendor and network service groups and with new types of library consortia. As a vital link between the local library and regional and national services, state networks can help identify critical issues, promote rational and economic network development from network suppliers and, at the local level, encourage effective network services to library users.

* * *

David Kaser

Thank you very much Barbara. I'm sure that all of us here can understand why we consider ourselves so fortunate in the State of Indiana to have Barbara with us.

* * *

I spent a little time in Japan recently and came across a practice which I was much impressed with. I'm going to use the Chairman's prerogative, here now in the next ninety seconds, to invite you to participate in this practice. What we do is we all stand up and we do some calisthenics. Now don't leave the room; don't leave your chair. Just stand up and unwind.

O.K., doesn't that make a big difference? Now, if you would have all got down and done a few pushups, you'd really be in better shape now!

Frank P. Grisham

Executive Director, SOLINET
Atlanta, Georgia

(Introductory Remarks by David Kaser)

Our next speaker here today was my closest professional associate from 1960 to 1968 when I was Director of the Joint University Libraries in Nashville, Tennessee and he was the Associate Director. At that time, the staff used to say that [Associate Director] meant "he was the only person who would associate with the Director." I don't know whether that's true or not but, at any rate, I can tell you that he wears exceedingly well. Following my Directorship there, he became Director and served for another twelve years.

So, between the two of us, we directed one of the country's oldest consortiums for more than two decades.

I think it probably says something that shortly after his retirement from that position, the place went bankrupt. At least it went out of business. (I'm sure it went bankrupt.)

I will say this about him, and this is something you probably won't find out in other sources; I don't find it in the Directory of American Libraries but, Frank is probably the only librarian you're ever going to meet who is—or at least was—a member of the Board of Directors of the Country Music Hall of Fame. How about that!

At this time, ladies and gentlemen, I'm pleased to give you the Director of SOLINET, Mr. Frank Grisham.

* * *

Greetings from SOLINET, the Southeastern Library Network, a non-profit membership cooperative of 318 members from ten states, which had its origin in the early 1970s. A few of you in this room were involved with the beginnings of the SOLINET network through the Association of Southeastern Research Libraries (ASERL). Those efforts have come to fruition in a variety of contributions through the programs of SOLINET.

We now have twenty-six full-time staff members. We are governed by an eleven-member Board of Directors elected by the membership; four of these are representatives from the ASERL contingency. We broker OCLC services, of course, with great pride. In addition, we have developed our own technical capability with the enhancement of software from the Washington Library Network, and we offer to our members a technical capability that is known by the trade name of "LAMBDA." We are now moving into new areas like retrospective conversion, service to small libraries, conservation/preservation, and the like.

I must preface my remarks by acknowledging that I am relatively new to the networking enterprise. My transition from a research library director to a network directorship has been both enjoyable and challenging. While I may lack the sophistication of such colleagues as those with whom I share the podium today, I am honored indeed that someone was willing to ask this new person to speak.

Where from here? No one really knows for sure. You may ask, "You mean after all these years and all this effort and all this money that we have put forth, we still don't know for sure where we are headed?" Right. We do have a few short-term benchmarks and goals that many of us looked for in earlier days, and those have served us well. Many of us hoped to have some kind of blueprint superimposed on us from on high, so that we would not have the responsibility, the accountability, and the anguish of deciding our own futures. Perhaps some of us would rather be told how to organize ourselves than to grapple with it ourselves. Perhaps it would be easier that way, because we could blame others for the failure; but no one has had the ability nor the courage nor felt it wise to devise such a master plan. For that, we are much better off. Why do I say that? First, I don't believe we could ever agree on a master plan. Barbara Markuson earlier discussed the difficulties of decision-making as a group process. These do not indicate our inability to work together, but simply reveal the complex issues we face. Secondly, we would all have sat on our hands and waited until the master plan was in place and would have done nothing in the meantime. Thirdly, no entity is in place which has the political or economic base to pull off such a feat as a master plan.

So the networks represented in this symposium and others around

FRANK GRISHAM: "In botany, most healthy plants spring from the soil, with a strong, deeply-embedded root system from which they gather nutrients. In networking, growth which emerges from a 'grassroots' need and maintains those roots will be stronger and better able to respond to the needs of the user. On the other hand, movement or structure superimposed from above is 'wrong-headed,' because it may be based on theory rather than on real needs and resources."

the country have "sort of emerged," which may be best for all of us, because growth from underneath is growth in the right direction. In botany, most healthy plants spring from the soil, with a strong, deeply-embedded root system from which they gather nutrients. In networking, growth which emerges from a "grassroots" need and maintains those roots will be stronger and better able to respond to the needs of the user. On the other hand, movement or structure superimposed from above is "wrong-headed," because it may be based on theory rather than on real needs and resources.

What has emerged is an array of diverse networks that must be examined diligently to find their commonality. But it is there; and those common elements should not simply be "linked to Dublin"—or, for that matter, to Olympia or Stanford or Toronto. The commonality is best described by acknowledging the fact that underneath the regionals—in fact, nourishing and supporting them—is their life blood and foundation. The commonality is the user. The sooner we acknowledge our commonality by looking in that direction (that is, toward the user), the quicker we will understand our roles.

I, therefore, come to the first of several paradoxes. Regional networks might best find themselves by losing themselves in their memberships. Therein lies a fundamental and crucial problem for us. How do we who are in the network business creatively analyze and understand and then reflect in our programs the needs of our users? What is SOLINET's source of information as to what its members need and want and can afford? Therein lies a challenge. We have a tendency to sit in our ivory towers and, without realizing it, tell our members what we think they need and want—not belligerently nor intentionally sometimes, but simply because we have not mastered the art of listening, communicating, and linking our programs to the real needs of the users. But that strategy is too much like the gimmicks of big business: inventing a product and then creating and artificial need for it.

One dimension of the problem that I'll not have time to explore in this presentation today lies in the frequent inability of our member libraries to determine and understand the needs of the patrons. I acknowledge that, as a library director, I encountered that problem; and although I worked diligently with my staff, we never developed a systematic methodology for identifying users' needs. So through all these levels of frustration from national utilities through regional networks to the ranks of the network members, we have a devas-

FRANK GRISHAM: "We have a tendency to sit in our ivory towers and, without realizing it, tell our members what we think they need and want, not belligerently nor intentionally sometimes, but simply because we have not mastered the art of listening, communicating, and linking our programs to the real needs of the users. But that strategy is too much like the gimmicks of big business: inventing a product and then creating an artificial need for it."

tating gap between the patron and the network program. The formulation of an answer would require another full symposium, so I'll leave that for another time. But let me oversimplify with what may seem a trite suggestion: that we establish a patrons' council as a way of relating directly to the users of information in our program development. Your response, and I can see it on your faces, is that the individual libraries should reflect the needs of the library members, and the national utilities should reflect the needs of the regional and state networks. For after all, this hierarchical pattern is found at work in such successful ventures as marketing in the business world, responsibility in the church (from God through the bishop to the member of the local church), and in the politics of the Democratic and Republican parties. Besides, if we did not have the middleman, many of us would be without jobs. Seriously, how do we get the needs of the scholar in the Baudelaire Studies Center at Vanderbilt, as well as those of the garage-mechanic-turned-genealogist in rural Tennessee, reflected in our programs? We have not lost the ability to represent the patron; for I fear we have never mastered it. Until we establish the linkage and creatively direct our programs by looking toward the patron, we will falter. Therefore, I suggest a second paradox.

By looking back at the needs of the user, we can look forward to a clearer understanding of our roles as networks. We have had a little problem in acknowledging the fact that we are a diverse group. That is good. Just as our patrons and resources differ, so do our network structures and services differ. Let us hope we have laid to rest the once heralded theory that we should all be alike in networking. Any effort to place us in a common mold should be resisted, for it would be nothing short of disastrous. So let us not dwell on this subject, for fear someone will want to resurrect that outdated concept, but simply conclude that observation by adding paradox number three.

Within our diversity, we will find our singleness of purpose. I come from Herschel Walker country, where it is important to know whose team you play on. In fact, it is not as important to know what game you are playing as it is to know who your teammates are. The regional networks have made much of their OCLC, RLG, and WLN relationships; and they should. However, one of the more interesting recent developments is the discussion going on among these regional and state networks as to how they may add another dimension to their programs through alliances with one another. As one network finds a common need and complementary resources with

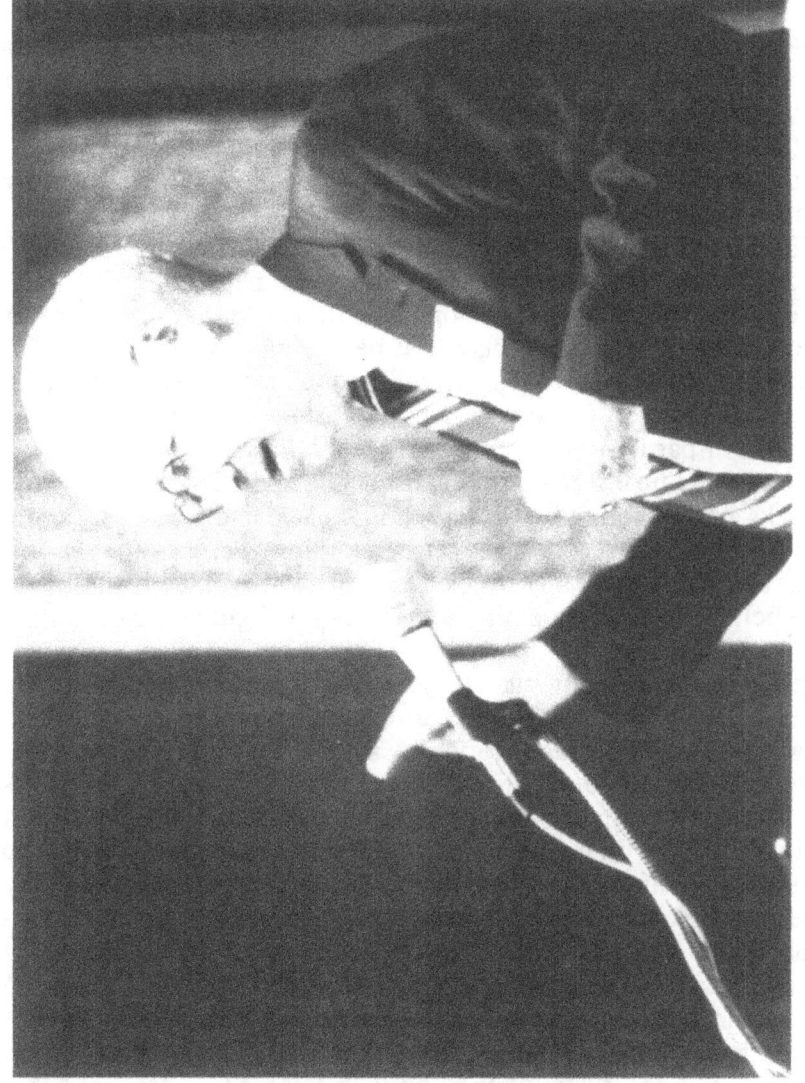

FRANK GRISHAM: "We have not lost the ability to represent the patron; for I fear we have never mastered it."

another network, new services and lateral relationships will emerge. The strict hierarchical pattern will begin to blur in this process, as will our strictly geographical identities. Geography will still set some limits, but it will also open up new options. However, the most important factor lies in an organizational theory. The closer you are to the action—that is, to the user—the greater the opportunity is for cooperative service. So I see a new and welcome phenomenon evolving on the scene: lateral program developments among the networks who have similarity in their purposes, their roles, and their goals. These factors will lead us to work together, not to detriment of the utilities, but (let us hope) cooperatively with the utilities, encouraged by the utilities. This leads me to paradox number four.

Those who join ranks with their neighbors will be more able to stand alone. Better communication among the networks will lead to more thoughtful program development. Resource sharing is a major topic among librarians; so should it be among "networkers." Cooperative program development will help us meet members' needs more effectively and use our members' dues and fees more efficiently. All participants in this area should be winners.

Now let us turn from the general to the specific, as I focus my remarks on the following observations that come from only eight months of experience in regional networking. Perhaps these comments are the result of a naive idealism that will eventually dissipate. But I believe these are the directions which will guide networking in the near future.

First, state and multi-state structures will prevail. You say, "So what? I didn't come all the way to Champaign to hear that." You knew that. Program identification by state is a natural phenomenon. Right now some of our states in the Southeast have great problems even with sending their monies across state lines. The state entity already exists. We do much as a state and with pride, and we shall do more. Multi-state structures will not have it so easy, because they are expendable in some program areas. That is a warning to us in regional networks. Middlemen can always be sacrificed, especially if they increase costs without adding value to services. Unless the middleman can identify a dependency role or offer a unique program, his days are numbered.

My second observation has to do with microcomputers, and that is covered well in the literature and elsewhere in our discussions here today. Microcomputers will have as great an impact on our programs and, in turn, on our culture as has television. I do not think we have properly anticipated the effects the micros will ultimately have on individual institutions as well as on networks. We all must carefully assess their potential and plan for their application.

Third, distributed processing will inevitably become the concept that shall bring a most dramatic change to our current relationships. The old theory, that we must push as much as possible out toward the user, will prevail. We will have to download some of our services and link them. A key element in this process will be service to small libraries. This can become a major responsibility for the regionals if they are willing to assume it. We at SOLINET plan to make this service a major and unique component of our future programs. It will be a simple and low-cost service for the many small libraries that cannot justify the service of the national utilities. Regionals can provide a less expensive and slightly less elaborate service that will greatly benefit those users who cannot afford to tie to the national utilities or to do it all themselves. So I see SOLINET with its technical capability providing a service to the small libraries that will be a unique, important contribution, though full of problems and challenges.

Resource sharing will be the keynote in the regional programs. It will first take the form of regional and state programs of collections development (as has already occurred in some areas), then in document delivery, and then it will move on into such areas as conservation/preservation and the like. We in the Southeast have great hopes of developing such programs. Various forms of resource sharing will be particularly attractive to the medium and large library. As regionals work to facilitate resource sharing programs, the networks may become competitive with one another. I welcome competition as a regional, because as the networks compete with one another for members or users, cooperation may evolve, since no network can meet all needs of all users. This competition will be to the benefit of the libraries, since it will enforce cost containment and will provide options.

Lastly, through gateways and linkages and other technical advances yet to be developed, we will someday wake up to the fact that we have been sharing data without realizing it. If nothing else does it, the new technologies that are available to us will force us to recognize the fact that our data is going to be shared. I remember well the days at Vanderbilt when we developed an access control

FRANK GRISHAM: "our greatest obstacle to progress and cooperation in networking is not in the economic or technical realms, but is in the human problems that abound."

system, which forced patrons to register their presence in the library, in order to provide management information. Those graduate students in engineering took great delight in beating the system and could do it with little trouble. Similarly, the advent and widespread use of photocopying machines initially seemed a dangerous, uncontrollable phenomenon. The advent of microcomputers and linkage capabilities, combined with the technical knowledge of this generation, is likely to result in the sharing of data whether we like it or not. These disparate systems will have the potential of being linked; and I can only hope that our surprised looks will turn into smiles and that we will look at what is happening to us as further opportunity for cooperation rather than as an obstacle.

This leads me to the final point I wish to make, and that is that our greatest obstacle to progress and cooperation in networking is not in the economic or technical realms, but is in the human problems that abound. Even in a limited area such as the Southeast, one encounters serious problems in reflecting and coping with the politics of states and local networks. Those difficulties will be greatly compounded as we try to address these issues on a national scale. I am nonetheless excited about the future of networking in the SOLINET region and across the nation; for I believe that, by attending to the paradoxes and driving forces I have mentioned, we can insure that the growth which emerges will be responsible and mutually beneficial.

* * *

David Kaser

Thank you very much, Frank. It certainly is a pleasure to be working with you again, even for such a short time.

I think you can see how working with Frank Grisham on a very, very close (minute to minute, hour to hour) basis—not only day to day, week to week, month to month—enabled me not only to learn a great deal in the way of facts from Frank, but also in the way of wisdom (which is perhaps, more important).

Frank did recognize the thinking of the planning group for this conference, when he pointed (or implied) that there were speakers both from the East and West of the—well, he didn't call it anything—the "Smith and Wesson" line, I think we call it. We have also speakers from the North and South of the "Grits" line.

Laima Mockus
Executive Director, NELINET
Newton, Massachusetts

(Introductory Remarks by David Kaser)

Our next speaker comes from the oldest of regional networks—she's not the oldest, the network is the oldest!
Previous to her work with NELINET, she served in both public and academic libraries in New York and New England.
She now brings us the perspective of NELINET, Mrs. Laima Mockus.

* * *

Speculation on the future of networking is a consistently popular and frequently controversial pastime. If past experience is assumed to be a fairly good partial indicator of the future, then it's safe to assume that networking will continue to be a hot topic in the year 2000.

Richard De Gennaro reminded us in June of 1979 that "library networking is still in its infancy." As a dynamic problem-solving process as well as an organizational model, the prognosis for "library networking" to survive turbulent teens is good—in New England and elsewhere—based on the rapid changes of recent years.

NELINET was originally established as a program of the New England Board of Higher Education (NEBHE), an interstate agency created by legislative compact in the 1950s. The purpose of NEBHE was to provide greater educational opportunities and services among residents of the six New England states: Maine, New Hampshire, Vermont, Connecticut, Massachusetts and Rhode Island.

The focus of NELINET (the New England Library Information Network) from its earliest days was: cooperative library automation as a means of enhancing access to regional collections. Under the initial leadership of the six state university library systems, NEL-

INET's membership grew to include other major libraries during the late 1960s. Grant funds were obtained to study the feasibility of automated cataloging and subsequently, offline batch processed card production was tested locally for the participating libraries.

In 1972, NELINET established its link with OCLC when Dartmouth College became the first member to initiate online shared cataloging via a dedicated phone line to Ohio. Within a year, 28 NELINET libraries were online with OCLC. Today there are over 240 NELINET OCLC users with several hundred other libraries participating via Processing Centers.

NELINET's mission has not changed significantly during the course of its history. The network's purpose has continued to be one of serving as the focal point for the achievement of cost effective library automation through shared resources. The network's Annual Report of 1972 stated that:

> in general, NELINET's objectives grew from two simple ideas: first, that several libraries working together on an interstate or regional basis could take significant steps toward solving some basic financial and service problems which face them; second, that some of the solutions to these problems would result in significant reductions in the rate of cost increases which face each library administrator at budget time.

As membership grew rapidly during the 1970s to include public and special libraries as well as other academic libraries, changes in network governance, technical planning and finances followed.

Governance needs, due to growth in size and aspirations during the 1970s, provided the impetus to separate from NEBHE in 1978 to become an independently incorporated, not for profit network. The former Executive Committee, an advisory group subordinate to the NEBHE Board of Directors, became the chief governing body of NELINET, Inc.

Since then, the NELINET Board of Directors has consisted entirely of elected representatives from voting member institutions. Although no formal requirements exist to elect Board members according to geographic, library type or library size criteria, in practice each Nominating Committee attempts to present a balanced slate of candidates. Eligibility for election to a three year term as a Board member provides an opportunity for each voting member

LAIMA MOCKUS: "Speculation on the future of networking is a consistently popular and frequently controversial pastime. If past experience is assumed to be a fairly good partial indicator of the future, then it's safe to assume that networking will continue to be a hot topic in the year 2000."

library to fully participate in and influence the legal, financial and service policies of the organization. Annual and regional voting member meetings provide further opportunities for representation of multi-type library perspectives.

Ten years ago participation in a centralized system offered the best opportunity for cost savings. Shared access to a single database of bibliographic information meant decreased duplication of staff effort in cataloging and in locating bibliographic information; reduced backlogs, materials processing time and per unit costs, and the benefits of standardized data formats.

The cooperative aspect of OCLC participants was visibly evident as catalogers willingly entered their data in hopes of finding, at first-pan, another user contributed record to help solve a tricky local cataloging chore. During the mid-70s system restrictions, quality control issues and the sometimes slow pace of our enhancements evolved into a catch-22 OCLC user relationship. As librarians became convinced they would no longer want to be without OCLC, they also became increasingly vocal in expressing frustration with system limitations. Libraries frequently turned to their networks in seeking common solutions to complement and supplement OCLC services.

Aside from the many good efforts initiated by OCLC in response to user needs, many networks, including NELINET, planned services calculated to satisfy reginal needs.

In fiscal year 1976, NELINET started an archival tape service whereby each member's OCLC activity was stored centrally for future use by individual libraries. Until last year the millions of records in this databank were paid for through general network revenues with each library bearing direct expenses only when individual library extractions were requested. As members increase COM and online catalog development, fewer need to use this central storage and tape maintenance service. A direct annual participants assessment has been initiated allowing reduced overhead surcharges.

The centralized tape service was initially also planned as a core regional database which could be loaded at NELINET to provide subject access, reduced telecommunications costs and other desirable services. NELINET hired highly qualified systems staff, entered protracted negotiations with OCLC concerning installation of a remote communications processor (RCP), moved into larger quarters and planned a strategy for testing the feasibility of an online regional database capable of meeting local library needs.

LAIMA MOCKUS: "The ability to mutually recognize and successfully respond to changed circumstances is evidence that networking works if member needs and constraints are heard and met."

During this period it became apparent that though technically feasible, a single centralized regional database was no longer an economically attractive option. Commercially available circulation systems, OCLC system enhancements and newly developed automated systems provided lower cost options to member libraries. Without outside network funding the financial burden of supporting a large scale single project would fall squarely on libraries whose budgets in many cases were already being strained.

Collectively, the membership, Board and staff responded to a changing technological and financial environment by refocusing our priorities. The ability to mutually recognize and successfully respond to changed circumstances is evidence that networking works if member needs and constraints are heard and met.

Reorganization during FY 1982 resulted in reaffirming our role as primarily an OCLC broker network providing marketing, training, and technical assistance to OCLC participating libraries at affordable rates.

What are some of the advantages of networking through service brokers such as NELINET? The answer includes savings in actual dollars and staff time, the introduction of new technology and the continued technical assistance and training opportunities.

Savings in technical processing costs due to the introduction of OCLC include the reduction and/or elimination of backlogs, the ease of retrieving cataloging copy online, and the fast turnaround time for receipt of catalog cards. Expensive acquisitions are thus made rapidly available for public use. Savings in online information retrieval for reference use amount to thousands of dollars for the network's users through participation in group discount programs with BRS, DIALOG and NYTIS database vendors. More effective professional staff distribution throughout departments has been possible in many NELINET Libraries due to the training of paraprofessionals to use online services. The negative effects of staff reductions through attrition or layoffs have in some cases been more easily absorbed because of the existence of online systems in a member library.

For many libraries, an OCLC broker network provided the first introduction to an automated system. The ease with which new technology was accepted was due in part to the network's ability to smooth the initial training and hands-on terminal experience. User guides, exercises and demonstrations of printers and other attachments were also provided. As member library staff became experienced and comfortable with OCLC, circulation and information

LAIMA MOCKUS: "The continuing support provided by a service broker network through technical assistance, daily trouble-shooting, newsletters, technical documentation and training is among the most significant contributions of networking. Permanent central staff support enables continued assistance in maximizing effective system use, adopting new features, training new staff, and exploring additional applications."

retrieval systems, networks have responded to requests for arranging demonstrations of COM and online catalog equipment and systems. In the future they are likely to move toward more microcomputer and related software introductory sessions.

Opportunities for sharing information about new technology are provided through regular user group meetings, such as NELINET's Library Technology Discussion Group. Other opportunities for sharing varying perspectives and needs among small and large libraries include workshops, meetings and demonstrations of services and equipment. The ability to interact with other multi-type libraries through NELINET over the years has benefited individual staff problem-solving efforts.

The continuing support provided by a service broker network through technical assistance, daily trouble-shooting, newsletters, technical documentation and training is among the most significant contributions of networking. Permanent central staff support enables continued assistance in maximizing effective system use, adopting new features, training new staff, and exploring additional applications.

This follow-up support aspect of library networking is also being recognized in other fields as a significant factor in the successful use of new technology. In the last two years there's been a growing recognition among large computer manufacturers and retail computer chains that support and technical assistance must be provided after the point of sale. Too many instances of discouraged users because equipment does not readily perform as promised bites into pales and creates a separate and independent service industry. IBM, DEC and others are focussing on ongoing support for their products to avoid new owner complaints.

For the future, the network's objectives are to continue present services, introduce additional related services and expand current and new member usage.

Assumptions for the future include the recognition that each member must have flexibility to choose among NELINET programs those which complement other internal systems. Libraries with circulation systems may need frequent archive tape copies for updating such systems or online union lists of serials to pupport local cooperative agreements.

Flexibility to choose among programs and services means an increase in the variety of services to be made available. While shared cataloging and interlibrary loan are of major importance to most members, access to online acquisitions is equally important to a small number.

If past experience is truly a partial indicator of the future, what is the effect of the reorganization this network experienced in terms of predicting future networking roles? The ability to respond appropriately to a changing environment is a key measure of organizational success. The increasing financial constraints felt by member libraries and the proliferation of locally owned computer systems combined to point the way toward a different role for NELINET. Instead of fighting these trends, the network redirected its priorities successfully to concentrate on doing what it does best. As long as the networking process operates responsively, it will continue in new forms.

As member libraries increase their own use, knowledge and technical expertise of automated systems, regional networking serves to encourage multi-type library cooperation and communication.

As long as NELINET's goals continue to be the provision of services which assist member libraries to reach their own automation goals and which encourage mutual accessibility of resources, networking will continue to be a beneficial vehicle for supporting library efforts to meet their public service goals in the future.

* * *

(David Kaser - Morning Wrap-up)

Thank you very much, Laima, for that very helpful account from the view of New England.

* * *

It's five minutes until noon; I'm reminded of the story of the school teacher who was, on the first day of school, giving new students the instructions of the school and said, "If any of you have to go to the bathroom, just raise your hand." One little boy said, "Teacher, how does that help?"

Well, you don't have to raise your hands, all you have to do is go downstairs. You go out these doors and turn to the right, and you'll find a stairway going down to the restrooms.

In five minutes—also downstairs (not in the restroom, but on that

LAIMA MOCKUS: "If past experience is truly a partial indicator of the future, what is the effect of the reorganization this network experienced in terms of predicting future networking roles? The ability to respond appropriately to a changing environment is a key measure of organizational success . . . As long as NELINET's goals continue to be the provision of services which assist member libraries to reach their own automation goals and which encourage mutual accessibility of resources, networking will continue to be a beneficial vehicle for supporting library efforts to meet their public service goals in the future."

floor), in a place called the Alumni Room you will find buffet lines prepared to offer us lunch—four tables. They will offer lunch to anyone wearing a name tag, so if you've lost your name tag or thrown it away, you don't get lunch today.

See you at 1:30!

Introduction for Afternoon Session

David Kaser, Moderator

During the lunch hour, I was handed this note that's addressed to the photographers, and it says, "Please do not take pictures while the speakers are speaking—shoot them before they get to the platform."

We'll have three speakers (seriatim) between now and three o'clock. Then we will take a twenty minute break for coffee, and then go into a panel discussion from three-twenty until five o'clock.

Richard McCoy

President, RLG, Inc.
Stanford, California

(Introductory Remarks by David Kaser)

Our first speaker on this afternoon's session is the recently appointed President of the Research Libraries Group, Inc. which we affectionately call (in the library world) "RLG".

You know, linguists say that you initialize things when the full length original term has an unpleasant aura about it (as when tuberculosis is reduced to "TB" and you have "DTs" and "EDs", and other unpleasant thoughts). I don't believe, however, that this necessarily applies to RLG, or OCLC, or NCLIS, or any of the other things we're going to be hearing about this afternoon.

Our first speaker this afternoon did most of his academic work—but not all—in Wisconsin, and has spent much of his career—but not all—in Wisconsin. He is a man of varied experiences, which are described briefly in your brochure so I won't go into detail here. I'll simply introduce him at this time. Your speaker, Dr. Rich McCoy.

* * *

First, I would like to tell you that I'm very delighted to be here. This is one of the first occasions on which RLG has allowed me to sally forth and speak to an audience as well informed and as large as this one. Frank told us earlier this morning about being very new to his particular assignment but I think I may have the record on that one. I've been at RLG something just over two and one-half months. The welcome that this Conference has prepared for me, as a newcomer, has been absolutely remarkable. I was amazed and delighted to find the RLG logo on the cover of the conference brochure. Some of you know our symbol, I'm sure. When moving to California such a very short time ago, I was a little surprised by the weather. I had been looking forward to that aspect of my move from Wisconsin and as those of you who watch the television news know, the winter in California has been an unusual one. They tell me they've now had two unusual ones, in sequence. I was very worried about that. I now live on the edge of the San Andreas fault and I see around me hillside homes sliding down onto the roadways and those along the ocean being washed away! I was very concerned until on the way here, coming through the Chicago airport, I saw a poster on the wall which I'm going to remember for a long time: It announced that all of the land *east* of the San Andreas fault is destined at any time to slide into the Atlantic Ocean. I think I'll be in position just to step in one direction or another, depending on how that comes out!

I want to speak to you about networking from the perspective of the Research Libraries Group and our perspective, I think, is somewhat different than those that have been represented earlier in the day. We are a partnership of about thirty research universities and I want to differentiate what we are doing from that which was discussed this morning. We were formed, not for the purposes of networking, but to support some common programs of sharing and cooperation among research libraries. The principle programs, I think you are familiar with: They are collection development, preservation, resource sharing, and providing access to each others' collections. The network, Research Libraries Information Network (RLIN), was developed as the necessary vehicle to implement the programs and permit them to serve member institutions. In addition to the foundation programs which I have mentioned, there are a number of special programs supporting East Asian collections, Art and Architecture, Music, Law and Medicine, for example.

RLIN, is by a number of measures, and I might add, by design, small. There are on the order of one hundred thousand organized libraries in the country and perhaps eight to ten thousand of them have access to some kind of automated network support, either from major networks, represented here or from other sources. Less than three hundred of those libraries are supported by RLIN and of that number, most are the libraries on the campuses of institutions which are RLG's owner-members.

By some measures, however, RLG is large. We have a fairly high proportion of the nation's largest and most significant research libraries. Our database is growing rapidly and today holds about nine million library specific bibliographic records. It will grow by more

RICHARD McCOY: "Our database is growing rapidly and today holds about nine million library specific bibliographic records. It will grow by more than four million records through the 'archive load' activity that we're undertaking this Spring and Summer. . . . The RLIN database is large by data processing measures and it occupies more than twelve billion bytes of data on magnetic storage (twelve gigabytes as the computer field calls that); with the activity underway this year, it will approach twenty gigabytes."

than four million records through the "archive load" activity that we're undertaking this Spring and this Summer. (We are loading the machine readable records created by our member institutions prior to the time that they participated in RLIN and records from a variety of other sources including the Government Printing Office, Medline, and others.) The RLIN database is large by data processing measures and it occupies more than twelve billion bytes of data on magnetic storage (twelve gigabytes as the computing field calls that); with the activity underway this year, it will approach twenty gigabytes. This places us in the club of "very large database" users, and brings us into confrontation with a series of new technological challenges. Because of this and other factors, we expect to be significantly challenged by technical development for all the years that we can foresee.

Many of you here are not users of, or familiar with RLIN and I'd like to tell you some things about it. It supports bibliographic records from the "decision records" when institutions are thinking about acquiring material through the acquistion process and eventually into full cataloging and does that as an intergrated activity. Once you have started the process, the record that you began with remains. Once you have entered an acquisition record, the material is in fact, locatable through searching just as if it had been cataloged. One does not have, of course, the advantage of full cataloging but basic information is there. The records are library specific and can be maintained by adding new or changed information as needs change, or when one decides to upgrade the cataloging information, it can be easily done. RLIN also provides notification which adds organization to the waiting game we all play—waiting for someone else to do the cataloging so we may copy it. As an RLIN user, it's possible to enter brief cataloging or acquisition level information and tell the system to let you know when someone else has done a better job; at that point you have the opportunity to upgrade your own cataloging. In addition, RLIN has been augmented this year with a number of preservation enhancements which let us record the condition of materials as they're cataloged. This information helps to identify which material is in urgent need of being preserved by filming or otherwise. RLIN also allows us to record the existence of master microfilm records, so that if someone has filmed an item, no one need do that again. These RLIN enhancements are an important part of the preservation program.

RLG is, of course, also very interested in providing wide access to information resources across our membership and to others. As individual institutions joined the partnership, they made commitments to open their resources to each other. If you're a scholar at one member institution you will be welcomed automatically into the library at another institution, also an RLG member. In addition, an extraordinary kind of sharing that, in many cases, didn't go on before, has developed in the interlibrary loan program. It has not only made accessible to a broad community of scholars, material of the New York Public Library and other collections that were not generally loaned, but it has also "taken off" in a fashion which is quite wonderful to watch: We set some standards which said that when an electronically transmitted loan request is issued, usually following a bibliographic search, that we'd like to have a return response within three days; a second standard said we'd like to have the materials physically delivered within nine days. We're achieving those standards routinely now and we're doing it because of a very positive competition and game which has developed. Member libraries are competing with each other to see who can do the best and quickest job of responding. Those that are doing so may be overworked, frazzled, and tired—but they're enthusiastic, too, as they seek the top spot on the ILL response statistics. If a request happens to arrive on a Friday afternoon, the respondents are quickly on the phone to their branch libraries, when needed, demanding an instant response so the statistics won't record the two days of the weekend. We've been very pleased and excited about both the responsiveness and the rapid growth of the ILL activity.

The RLIN network has been changing and growing during 1983 and I think you might like to know of some of the highlights. One of them is found in the preservation enhancements which I mentioned earlier; they are an essential tool in the support of RLG's preservation program. A second is an activity in support of the East Asian program, namely the availability of the "CJK" or Chinese, Japanese and Korean terminal cluster. We've had their terminals capable of entering all three languages (plus Roman characters) operating in our offices for some time, but this month marks the first installation for production use in member libraries. The Library of Congress will receive their terminals late this month and so will the Hoover Institute on the Stanford University campus. About a dozen institutions will be installing CJK terminals this year bringing for the first time, the benefits of automation to a field where this was not possible before, and bringing a new level of access of information to

RICHARD McCOY: "This is a critical time as we put these [CJK] terminals into the hands, not only of RLG staff (who have been terribly enthusiastic and excited about them) but into the hands of working catalogers and librarians—many of whom are encountering automation for the first time. Non-Roman support (a follow on to the CJK project) will soon bring other character sets into the system; these will include Cyrillic, Hebraic, Greek, and Arabic."

scholars of East Asian material. The terminals open-ended can deal ultimately with all of the characters of these languages. The CJK development brings automation to this field for the first time and simultaneously lets me tell you something about the nature of the RLG partnership. That kind of activity is not one to undertake as an exciting business prospect in which the intent is to sell lots and lots of the things. There are but a few thousand scholars who require access to East Asian materials in the vernacular, not including native speakers who will make use of the capability also. We have not developed the CJK capability because it's a business proposition but because it is a critical addition to an extremely important field of scholarship. RLG is very excited about this activity and we hope you'll watch it as it develops. This is a critical time as we put these terminals into the hands, not only of RLG staff (who have been terribly enthusiastic and excited about them) but into the hands of working catalogers and librarians—many of whom are encountering automation for the first time. Non-Roman support (a follow on to the CJK project) will soon bring other character sets into the system; these will include Cyrillic, Hebraic, Greek, and Arabic.

Another RLIN development for 1983 is an archives and manuscripts capability. This will bring automation support and newly defined standards of bibliographic control to that field which has not enjoyed it. We are particularly interested, even entertained when thinking about the experiences which RLG institutions will have, as scholars looking for material begin to find the archival material which they could never locate or identify before. Patrons will be asking for this material soon, and it's going to be an interesting challenge for the librarians who are not used to seeing it themselves. Another project we're very enthusiastic about at present is the Linked System Project in which we're applying evolving international standards and to the problem of interconnecting the networks of RLIN, the Library of Congress, and the Washington Library Network. We believe this will provide an important foundation on which to build toward a more general sharing of bibliographic information among all networks.

Some brief comments about content may be useful here: in addition to the databases on books, serials, films, maps, scores, and recordings that are in the main RLIN database, we support a variety of special databases, including the Avery index to Art & Architecture, the SCRIPIO index of Art Sales Catalogs, ESTC (the Eighteenth Century Short Title Catalog), and a new special database

RICHARD McCOY: "At Wisconsin, one forecast suggests that there will be seventeen thousand work stations by the end of the decade, a work station where ever there is a telephone today."

cataloging machine readable data files. A very important new file is the RLG Conspectus, an online searchable database documenting the strengths of existing collections and of collecting intensity across the various disciplines. This is an important tool to support our goals in the area of shared collection development. We hope the Conspectus will become a general tool for research libraries whether in RLG or not.

The theme today is "Networking—Where from Here?" I want to talk to you about today, tomorrow, and a little bit the-day-after-tomorrow. To a great extent, I've already talked about "today" from RLG's perspective by telling you about RLIN. I must first underscore the comments made earlier about the tremendous and rapid gains in technology which are delivering individual work stations, personal computers, or microcomputers into the hands of so many. The new technologies are also producing the related local area networks or "LAN's" which are interconnecting these devices, allowing them to communicate with each other and with other networks including, of course, those of the libraries. These developments are the source of what will happen in the networks of major research universities. Here are a couple of quick facts in areas that I'm familiar with. At Wisconsin, one forecast suggests that there will be seventeen thousand work stations by the end of the decade, a work station where ever there is a telephone today; that institution already has in operation and in place two broad-band high-speed local area networks. Wisconsin signed an order with one vendor for five thousand personal computers to be delivered over the next few years. You know about Carnegie-Mellon, I'm sure; it took a visionary lead which six other institutions have followed by requiring that all of the students coming to the campus have their own personal computer. They will pay for it in their tuition, use it for four years and take it with them when they leave. That's ok because it will be largely obsolete by that time anyway and newly arriving students will surely require a more powerful model! This is just another indication of the way in which the new technologies which most of us hadn't really recognized before two or three years ago are becoming ubiquitous. At Stanford there is a new program which will be most interesting to watch. RLG's facilities are on that campus so we can be particularly aware of what they do. The Stanford project called "TIRO" has just put IBM personal computers in the hands of 137 members of the humanities faculties. Most have elected to install their machines at home rather than in the office. The first major application, of course, is word processing or text editing, applications of enormous attractiveness to authors.

Public service librarians at some major universities across the country are still asking "Should we install ten or should we install twenty public service online catalog access terminals?" That question is probably obsolete as the new small machines will require a new question. The new question must be, "How are we possibly going to respond to the ten thousand machines that will be out there breaking down the "electronic doors" of the library to get access to a resource of extraordinary value, the bibliographic database?" Most universities are by now planning with a sense of great urgency for the new information technologies. That planning is generally going on off in one corner of the campus, involving the people in the computing centers and those in telecommunications. Typically, the librarians are not involved and this represents a very important issue for all of us and an important challenge for the network organizations that are represented here. We have to make the point that both are in the same business. The technology planners who are doing their urgent work need the libraries as much as the libraries need them. I listened in November to Steven Muller, the President of Johns Hopkins University, talking about these topics and he had some very interesting and provocative questions: "Will the library become the museum of the book?" "Can the library transcend its name?" The answers must be NO, the library won't become the museum of the book, and YES, it can and must transcend its name but there's much work to be done to make that possible and let me tell you some of the things RLG is doing about it.

RLG is working with its members on every available occasion and with our colleagues in the computing and technology area. We're working to build the bridges and the interconnections between those in the "new" information technologies and those I guess one could say, in the "old" information technologies; we need to come together and become a part of the same new system. We're hopeful that others like, for example, the EDUCOM organization, another consortium of universities will help in making this important link. We're working on the challenging Linked Systems Project with the Library of Congress and the Washington Library Network to find ways to interconnect our networks so that they can share information technically. We'll be moving late this year to the first application of that interconnection which will bring about a full sharing of authorities records.

A major activity at RLG is the Distributed Processing Study funded by the Carnegie Corporation. We're studying not just technology which is encouraging computing and data to move outward from the central location to local sites at our member institutions, for instance. Most importantly, we're studying the needs of our member institutions for integrated library services. We're looking also at the programs or national purposes for which we carry out our activity, for the economics of library networking is going to change drastically. Much more proportionally of the automated activity will take place and be paid for at individual institutions, and not at some central location like ours or others. We're taking a hard look at the process of transition which is going to have to be managed very carefully if we libraries wish to meet concurrently their local purposes, their shared responsibilities, and the national purposes which are reflected in RLG's programs.

There are about thirty owner-member institutions within the RLG partnership. About half of them already have substantial library automation activities on their own campuses. They are making major investments today in expanding, extending and building those systems; several are acquiring new systems that are being made available commercially. The emphasis in earlier systems was on circulation and serials control and check-in. That's changing and broadening. The emphasis is moving to things like acquisition and online catalogs. We're terribly excited about that and doing what we can to encourage the development. From this "today" situation, let's move quickly to "tomorrow." The development and acquisition of local library automation systems will clearly move from the specifically targeted systems that deal independently with particular areas of library activity, to integrated local host systems. Integration is absolutely essential to our field because it is essential to the library patron. The patron asks first, "Does it exist?" then, "Do you have it here?" If negative, the next question is "Is it on order?" and if not, "Does someone else have it and can I get it?" If you're more fortunate and do have the required item, the obvious question is, "Is it on the shelf?" Because these questions move you from one of the component automation systems into another one and because you don't want to do that by backing away from a green terminal and going over to a red terminal and starting anew; you must have a convenient and natural transition. We know as a result that the developing local library systems will indeed be integrated. They will deal in a single framework with circulation, serials, acquisitions, online catalogs, and other applications.

In the "tomorrow" activity, considerable dependence will still

70 *Library Networking: Current Problems and Future Prospects*

RICHARD McCOY: "In the 'tomorrow' activity, considerable dependence will still exist on work performed at some central site by a national network, particularly for those activities which require sharing. The 'day-after-tomorrow' will see a greater change. I expect a redefinition of 'library' in the minds of scholars at universities and elsewhere."

exist on work performed at some central site by a national network, particularly for those activities which require sharing. The "day-after-tomorrow" will see a greater change. I expect a redefinition of "library" in the minds of scholars at universities and elsewhere. I don't know whether that means they will use a different term like "information resource" into which the library is incorporated or whether they will think "library" and have in mind something quite different than most people think of today. Seen from an automation perspective, many functions that RLIN supports today will be carried out on a local integrated host. In this "day-after-tomorrow," or perhaps shortly after the end of the decade, it will be technically feasible and indeed quite likely that the full union catalog by then thirty or more gigabytes of information will be available to integrated local hosts at their local sites. It will not then be necessary to access a national network like RLIN for searching or copy cataloging. RLIN may cease to exist in the sense that we know it now. We're certain, however, that the programs which RLIN supports will still be very much present. There will remain a technical role in gathering together the information and records produced and prepared at various institutions, assembling and combining them, editing and formatting them, and then shipping them back periodically as a freshly updated database for the local integrated systems. We're very comfortable with that kind of development. I want, in fact, to take issue (soto voce) with comments made earlier in the day which held that it isn't quite clear how the future is going to develop. There are, of course, some very large question marks in a transition of this magnitude. I understand that, and I agree with it, but we're trying very hard to look at the things which we can personally forecast. We're looking at the inertia in what our members are already doing. We're looking at technology which is not dependent on some unexpected "break through", but at that which we can view and see today and which requires only an extrapolation of the development paths we've come to accept as normal. We're looking also at the needs of research institutions. With the results of this kind of study in hand, it will be our role *to make the future happen.* The way in which we will be making that future happen is to support orderly "distribution" to integrated local host systems. We will support a very much changed role for an RLIN network and will assume a new kind of responsibility for supporting those activities that can only be done on a widely shared basis and from a national platform.

We hope and plan for much more from the "day-after-tomorrow." Sharing must be much more general so that bibliographic records developed in one network or in one local system will not only be shared with other members of the same "club" but for the benefit of scholarship everywhere. An important role that all of you must have is to bring pressure to bear on the national networks so that we will have no choice but find ways around the political and economic obstacles which inhibit sharing and cooperation. The international connection will be more fully established on the "day-after-tomorrow." It's just beginning now and it is abundantly clear that the boundaries of scholarships are not geographic. When a scholar has completed a search of the material in their local library and extended that to the libraries of the nation, they must be able to go beyond that to look at material in other major libraries of the world. Research libraries in particular find that very important. Much of their acquisitions budgets and their materials are in foreign languages, and originate in other nations; greater cooperation with the major foreign libraries will soon become essential. Electronic document delivery will also be well established on the "day-after-tomorrow" with great potential that full text and not just bibliographic records will become standard on the communications lines. It will be an exciting future and a very challenging transition!

My time is up so let me close with a personal experience. My wife, Elizabeth, is a librarian (and that may have been one of my most important credentials for coming to the Research Libraries Group). Elizabeth has spent the last twenty years, more time than I like to think about, following my work at computing centers. She's very familiar with the application of computers to higher education, to government and to business and it was a curious experience for me as I introduced her to the things which RLG was doing. We have a terminal at home so we can access the network and do searching there. It's a wonderful experience to browse through the eighteenth century, for instance, with the rich kind of searching capabilities which RLIN offers. She thought about this experience for only a short time before deciding "This is the first time I've ever seen a computer do something useful!" Thank you.

* * *

David Kaser

Thank you very much, Dick, for that very exciting account from the viewpoint of RLG.

Rowland Brown

President and Chief Executive Officer,
OCLC, Inc.
Dublin, Ohio

(Introductory Remarks by David Kaser)

Our next speaker is the President and Chief Executive Officer of OCLC, Inc. in Dublin, Ohio. He was educated at Harvard and MIT, and has succeeded in a number of different walks of life—not the least of which was as a fighter pilot during World War II in the Marine Air Corps, and as a bomber pilot in the Korean War. His success, I think, is evinced by the fact that he is still with us. He attained the rank of Major.

He also has had a successful career in corporate law and industrial management. Certainly, this is the kind of success experience that we need in our major bibliographic utilities—Mr. Rowland Brown.

* * *

Good afternoon. I think what our Chairman was saying in his introduction was that I'm a survivor and in a way maybe that's the gist of some of what we're talking about today. Some people view the whole question of "Where are we going?" as "How do we survive?" rather than looking at the brave new world of opportunities.

I may have a somewhat unique position on this panel. There are at least four networks officially represented by their directors here today, networks that are part of OCLC's national network, brokering OCLC services to libraries. One said before I stepped up here, "Now I want to find out what you're going to do to us."

"Networking, Where From Here?" One is tempted to start with a couple of one-liners, not much different from Frank Grisham's,

"I wish I knew." We all think we know where we're going, but the options are so varied and so many changes are taking place around us that I think we'd also have to say very honestly that we don't know with certainty what the future holds for networks. We can only project based upon our present experience. In fact, we are all trapped by our present experience. St. Augustine once said—this is a paraphrase—"Time is a three-fold present: the present as we experience it, the past as a present memory and the future as a present expectation."

That reminds me of a story I heard recently about how we are trapped in terms of our perspectives and how we are conditioned to respond in certain ways. In the networking world we're all guilty of this and perhaps at times may be too defensive. A man was driving his sports car in the Italian Alps. (I don't know whether any of you have had the opportunity to drive in the Alps, but as soon as an Italian or Frenchman puts on his driving gloves and climbs in a car, he changes his character and becomes a Grand Prix competitor ready to challenge anyone.) He was whirling around these tortuous roads and suddenly, just before he came to a sharp blind turn, around the turn came another roadster. A woman in the car leaned out the window and shouted, "Pig! Pig!" He was startled, looked at her and put his head in the windstream and shouted back, "Sow!" Just then he turned the corner and ran into a three hundred pound pig in the middle of the highway. Sometimes we're not listening to what people are trying to tell us.

At OCLC these days we're trying very hard to listen, as well as to plan. While perhaps it's not exciting to you, I find it interesting and gratifying that the panelists seem to be agreeing quite a bit today. I listened with great interest and attention to Dick McCoy's projections of the future and where he sees RLG going. I must say, I would concur his prognostications in terms of the impact of local systems, integrated systems, personal computers, etc. and the changing role of national, state and local systems and indeed even libraries. We all are changing.

I'm sure all of you, as you have prepared a talk or a paper, have had an event occur or an article appear that provides you with a focal point. A couple of years ago it would have been a book by Toffler. Today it could be *Megatrends,* by John Naisbitt, which points up many of the trends that will impact on all of us, including networking. The April 1 issue of the *Library Journal* carried an article entitled, "Library Automation & Networking: Perspective on Three

ROWLAND BROWN: "While perhaps it's not exciting to you, I find it interesting and gratifying that the panelists seem to be agreeing quite a bit today."

Decades," which provides my focus today. The author, Richard DeGennaro, the distinguished librarian of the University of Pennsylvania, has had broad involvement in networking at all levels: as a former cataloging member of OCLC, as a member-director of RLG, as a participating member of PALINET and as a tapeloading member of OCLC.

It is interesting that a year ago the April 1 issue of the *Journal* carried an article entitled, "Networking. Who Needs it?" I mention this only to remind us all that the concept of networking, which has made tremendous contributions to the library scene in the United States, is constantly being challenged.

The thrust of DeGennaro's provocative article is that library automation and networking have gone through three different phases in the 60s, 70s and 80s. The first phase was characterized by early, "primitive" local systems and the beginnings of the multi-library bibliographic systems; the 70s were dominated by large, multitype and multipurpose library networks. The current decade, the 80s, DeGennaro contends, will be dominated by a return to local systems. These dominant trends in library automation, he correctly points out, were "shaped and driven by the cost and capabilities of the computer and communication technologies that were available at the time." While I would agree with his characterization of the broad trends and many of his observations, there are several conclusions with which I am in strong disagreement.

First of all, he contends that local systems will enable libraries to "regain much of the control over their own operations and decision-making that they gave up to the networks in the 1970s." My problem with this observation is that I don't believe that libraries ever lost or gave up control of their operations to networks. If they did, it wasn't because of either networking or OCLC or RLG; it was because of decisions within the library itself. Basically, what networks have done is supplement what libraries have been doing, not replace what they can and should be doing within the library.

Speaking for OCLC, I would assert that one of the strengths of OCLC's bibliographic system is that it enhanced and complemented the library's activities and neither took control nor stole options away from them. It enabled libraries to reduce costs of cataloging and improve the effectiveness of interlibrary loan activity while leaving them the opportunity to develop or purchase local systems to replace card catalogs and to automate circulation and other activities. Indeed OCLC has for a number of years planned to supplement its centralized online bibliographic service with local mini- and micro-based systems. I do not believe the OCLC member libraries ever lost control. On the contrary, they have gained more control over their operations, including costs.

DeGennaro contends that, "One of the hard lessons we are learning from our experience in the 1970s is that cooperation is difficult, time-consuming and expensive way to do something and the results are frequently disappointing." He goes on to say, "The general euphoria in favor of cooperation in networking that characterized the 1970s is over. The networks are going to have to compete with local systems and commercial vendors in the 1980s or they will lose their members and their financial base."

I suggest that no one who has studied collaborative efforts, from the time of the first prehistoric hunting party down to current library networks, ever believed that cooperation was easy. Working with machines is far easier than cooperating with other individuals, with human institutions and organizations. On the other hand, cooperation at its best is one of the hallmarks of civilization.

With regard to the euphoria DeGenarro refers to, I confess I have not witnessed it during my tenure at OCLC. Earlier, Dick McCoy observed that as a non-librarian this is his baptism with such a group. Also being a non-librarian, I experienced my library baptism at a meeting at SOLINET a few years ago, only a few days after I had joined OCLC. I was invited to a membership meeting at which the members had much on their minds and many concerns that related to both SOLINET and OCLC, and feelings ran strong. I don't know whether I am becoming a surrogate librarian by osmosis or by total immersion, but I felt I could easily have drowned at that meeting and it certainly wasn't in a sea of euphoria.

I strongly contend that the original mission of OCLC (reducing the rate of rising costs of library bibliographic services and providing the means for libraries to share resources) is just as valid today as it was at OCLC's inception in 1967. In many ways, as we look at the statistics, OCLC has probably exceeded the fondest hopes of its originators in Ohio. But we are witnessing constantly rising expectations as we approach our earlier established goals, and whatever we achieve pales in comparison to what our users have grown to expect. Despite the plethora of technical options available to libraries and their patrons from both not-for-profit and commercial institutions, diminishing financial resources and competition for these scarce funds make it imperative that we build cost effectively

ROWLAND BROWN: "I suggest that no one who has studied collaborative efforts, from the time of the first prehistoric hunting party down to current library networks, ever believed that cooperation was easy. . . . I contend further that if the 70s were indeed the golden age of cooperation, the 80s will have to be the platinum age, in terms of resource sharing."

upon and complement collaboration. We must not ignore or destroy what has been painstakingly created and nurtured through networking.

I contend further that if the 70s were indeed the golden age of cooperation, the 80s will have to be the platinum age, in terms of resource sharing. As I view the economy and the national and state budgets, the revenues that will be required for pensions, social security, defense, health services and interest on all forms of debt are going to eat up a great deal of the nation's resources at a time when revenue growth will be slow and taxpayer support will be reluctant. Education, in all its forms, will be hard pressed, despite a growing awareness of the national dimension of its difficulties. The gross national product is likely to grow more slowly in the near future than in the past, and that's not an environment for euphoria or of enthusiasm for providing financial resources for redundant or suboptimized systems. It is an environment that calls for careful planning of how we coordinate and cooperate and build upon what we already have.

This in no way implies that we as networks can afford not to be responsive, soundly governed and managed, cost effective and capable of adapting to a changing environment. Our environment has changed and continues to change in many and subtle ways. Paradoxically, new technology allows and encourages new and closer relationships among libraries while at the same time it permits greater independence. As I view the library ecosystem, I see networking, already a bewildering maze of interdependencies, becoming yet more labyrinthine, with increasing options made possible, indeed required, by changing technology and with increasingly computer-literate faculty and populace.

We are at once turning our attention inwardly to our own institutions and at the same time outwardly toward a national system. While moving to take advantage of local options, we are becoming increasingly aware of the need for national and even international standards, of expanded resource sharing capabilities, and of a national bibliographic system that can remain economically viable in a rapidly changing environment that allows for, and even rewards, what I would term potential systems anarchy. Indeed, as is pointed out in the discussion of networks in *Megatrends*, as we become increasingly dependent upon technology, we become equally concerned about how we link with other people to accomplish our needs through this personal sharing.

In any case, at OCLC we believe networking encompasses resource sharing and other services including, but not certainly limited to, electronic services. We frequently overlook the vast resources that are made available through networking that are not computer or technology dependent. Indeed, in the case of RLG, it is the programmatic goals which they have developed and are supporting, and which require inter-institutional collaboration for their fulfillment, with which OCLC and OCLC libraries find the greatest identity of interest. It is these programmatic efforts—efforts that transcend systems dependency—for which we must find cooperation solutions that are more than mere systems linkage.

Another eye-catching—or mind-catching—observation in DeGennaro's article is his admonition that, "While networks were created by libraries to serve certain needs and services that are best provided collectively, networks should not be given or allowed to take on functions and services that are better done locally or by other means." I would heartily agree and would go even further and say that, except in minor and special circumstances, networks should not develop and take on services that are not cost effective or capable of being financially supported on a continuing basis by their members. OCLC's planning and its systems architecture is based on this premise and it has frequently been only because of the leverage of its large total critical mass of institutions that the unique needs of various library groups within the larger membership could be accommodated and justified.

By the same token, I suggest that both foundations and individual libraries apply the same careful criteria in evaluating proposed new systems and opportunities. There is, indeed, a growing range of new opportunities for both single institutions and groups of institutions, as well as for individuals, to access and manage information and materials in new ways, more opportunities than most libraries and institutions are in a position to finance or maintain.

I'm not convinced that collaboration or networking will diminish in importance. Resources are going to be scarce, and while the cost of computers, memory and peripherals are coming down, the cost of software, development and maintenance are not and operating budgets are becoming leaner. Networks can and do help in controlling these costs.

Yes, the 80s will introduce increasing options for individual libraries, for clusters of libraries, and for local, state and regional networks. Mini- and micro-computers with increasing capacity and high density storage will eventually allow large union catalogs to be resident in many institutions and on many campuses, and there will be new terrestrial and satellite communication alternatives to lower communication costs. All of this will impel the increasingly computer-literate public to attempt to multiply the options. Thus, I see the 80's as continuing the trend towards the development of library automation systems that not only provide local online public catalog access, circulation, acquistions and other backroom services but are also integrated with strong national systems.

Contrary to DeGennaro's observations (and unlike RLG's original architecture), OCLC has never seen our online bibliographic system as a substitute for a local online catalog. They are multi-level functions with some at a local or clustered level and others at higher or more centralized level, depending upon the economics and the database needs, all of which ideally will someday be transparent to the user. We have never tried to develop a substitute for the local online catalog in whole or in partitioned form. That's one of the reasons we have never had one of the most desirable features that RLIN has: subject search capability. But with the availability of local online catalogs capable of sophisticated online searching, I expect that most people will do their primary searching on the local catalog and then go to a second- or third-tier database. I hope that, not too far in the future, OCLC will have a capability of subject search on a part of its total database but for what I would consider to be supplementary searching, not to replace the local online catalog.

No one would concur more readily than we do with DeGennaro's observation that, "We will never have a finished total integrated library system because we will never be satisfied to freeze the system when we know that further improvements will always be possible." Indeed, in an organization like OCLC the real problem is to pluck any system out of development prior to the time that the development department is ready to allow it to leave the womb. Systems developers will never be satisfied because there will always be room for further refinement. If you are not prepared to introduce a system before it is considered "complete" you'll never produce any system in a timely and cost-effective manner. Nevertheless, the state-of-the-art systems that do exist now, or will be available in the coming months, will, I believe, meet most libraries' or clustered libraries' current needs.

We see local, centralized, national and rapidly developing international networks integrating in a manner that takes into account the changing economies of scale which are facilitating local options, flexibility of local needs, and resource sharing among an ever-widening and diverse body of institutions. This, I suggest, requires more than mere linkage. The emergence of state resource-shared systems, which I referred to earlier, primarily directed to public and school libraries, will present opportunities and challenges, for both OCLC and the existing state and regional networks. We feel that the major change in the 80s with respect to networking will be as the rising activity of state databases that Frank Grisham and others referred to earlier, and how they are integrated into the larger and existing systems. Also, in many cases there will be increasing activity in geographical and traditional resource sharing. We also believe that state networks must somehow take into account the interstate relationships that already exist among institutions in many parts of the country.

We believe that the central focus of the latter part of this decade will not be on the bibliographic services, collection, preservation, circulation management and other important central functions, but will gradually shift to the user's needs and to services that make it easier and more convenient for users to access information they need where they want it, when they want it, and at a cost that is perceived as affordable by the user, the institution, or society, depending upon who is to bear the cost. We must never delude ourselves that information is free; it is only made freely available by public or institutional policy—as issue for another forum.

In this scenario, not only will networks change, but so will libraries and the institutions of which they are a part. I strongly believe that increasing computer literacy of our younger population, augmented by the fact that many of our educational institutions (over a hundred already, and I would guess that figure will double within a year or so) will be requiring or financing computers for all of their students, and their faculty, will have as profound an effect on libraries as will advances in technology. The rapid proliferation of personal computers and software packages and the rising expectations and demands for options by the patron will be the biggest factor in the systems architecture of the future. Electronic document delivery and electronic access to abstracts and partial or full text will probably become a major area of activity for OCLC and for others. In fact, if I were to hazard a guess, I would say that in the future this activity may overshadow OCLC's bibliographic system. I note that DeGennaro makes a similar observation.

ROWLAND BROWN: "We must never delude ourselves that information is free; it is only made freely available by public or institutional policy—an issue for another forum. . . .I strongly believe that increasing computer literacy of our younger population,. . . will have as profound an effect on libraries as will advances in technology."

What about OCLC? How will we address these changes? First of all, I think we do not fit DeGennaro's characterization of a utility (a term I dislike): "The largest of the utilities . . . are in danger of becoming increasingly inflexible and unresponsive. . . . The utilities tend to be under-capitalized and over-governed." Now that's a chicken that's come home to roost! Back in 1980 at the SOLINET meeting I mentioned earlier as my baptism, I observed that OCLC was under-capitalized, over-governed and under-managed, and I also went on to say that we tended to confuse governance with marketing research. These were valid observations at that time, but I can happily say that I don't believe any of those conditions exist today and haven't for some time. The Users Council of OCLC, a unique institution in cooperative member governance, has become increasingly effective and supportive. OCLC's Board has assumed a policy-making, not a management, role and OCLC's management has broadened its skills and its capacity for communicating, including listening and decision-making. (Some people mistake merely saying something to someone for communicating.) We no longer confuse governance with marketing, or wish-lists of members with genuine, in-depth market research of what is needed and will be supported. The unique structure of our Board and a clear delegation of powers by them to professional management, a broad mission statement approved by our Users Council, and constant input from a broad range of user advisory groups, technology advisors, etc., permits us to be flexible and responsive to changing conditions and opportunities. We're developing more effective working relationships with the twenty supporting networks that enable OCLC to provide services to our members in an efficient and cost-effective manner, and we are defining mutual, complementary roles for OCLC and those networks. Our recent Newsletter discussed a very important "relationship document" that the networks and we have worked out.

As for being under-capitalized, our net worth, or capital, stood at approximately $23 million on March 31, with a sound debt/equity ratio and the capacity to borrow from traditional sources as we have in the past. I would not consider that to be under-capitalized, although perhaps DeGennaro had other systems in mind.

Our terminal population stands at slightly over 5,000, with more than 700 additional dial access users. As of March 31, we had 4,200 member libraries and are serving some 3,000 more indirectly. During the month of March, we had 47 million transactions; there

ROWLAND BROWN: "Yes, I think networks are being challenged and need to change to reflect a changing environment and priorities. . . .I am convinced that the networks we know will meet their challenges."

were 14 days during which we had over 2 million transactions a day. Prior to January, we had never had a 2 million-transaction day. So much for health and capacity. Suffice it to say that we are in a position to be a constructive leadership force for all of the various networks, libraries and users.

We are expanding into Western Europe, South America and Mexico and we'll be reporting on some exciting developments in this regard later this year. You already know that we are in the course of restructuring our systems architecture and our telecommunications. We will be introducing a powerful integrated local system at the ALA meeting, and our research and development is directed towards various forms of patron access to information.

As for becoming inflexible and unresponsive, I believe that it would be more accurate to say that many of our members are concerned that we are changing too fast and creating too many waves in a fairly conservative environment.

Yes, I think networks are being challenged and need to change to reflect a changing environment and priorities. But I also believe they are well positioned to assist libraries, their institutions and their patrons to take full advantage of the myriad of exciting opportunities created by new technologies and to do so in a cost-effective manner. I am convinced that the networks we know will meet their challenges.

* * *

David Kaser

Thank you for that very informative presentation.

Toni Carbo Bearman

Executive Director
National Commission on Libraries and Information Science
Washington, D.C.

(Introductory Remarks by David Kaser)

I find that in my attempt to be funny, I seem to have been impairing the future archives of the library world. We won't have pictures of the rest of this conference if I don't retract—I made that little note up. I really didn't. . .

Our last speaker today is one who is, perhaps, better known—longer known, at any rate—in the library community. A well known figure in libraries and information science, both in this country and abroad; and most recently, of course, known for her Executive Directorship of the National Commission on Libraries and Information Science, Dr. Toni Bearman.

* * *

Good afternoon. It is a great pleasure to be back in Champaign and to participate in this symposium on networking. Flying into O'Hare yesterday brought back very special memories for me. It was in a hotel at O'Hare in September of 1980 that I was selected for my current position.

I have subtitled my presentation today, "One Individual's View from Washington," both to emphasize the fact that my comments reflect my own personal views and not necessarily those of the Commission or of the U.S. Government, and also to point out that my perspective is from a small town called Washington, D.C. I do not work for a network and never have, although I have been active in the networking field for many years.

My perspective on networking is somewhat different, and perhaps a bit broader, than those of some of the previous speakers. Jim Haas of the Council on Library Resources, Inc., has defined a library network as "a system of computer and communicating capabilities established and organized to serve a purpose of value to libraries and their users."[1] I feel this definition restricts networks to library networks and places too much emphasis on the hardware. Personally, I prefer the definition proposed by Ward Shaw of the Colorado Alliance of Research Libraries: A system composed of independent components acting together to accomplish some mutually beneficial purpose.[2]

The key phrases are "system," "independent components" and "mutually beneficial purpose." Of course, informal networks among institutions and individuals have existed for centuries. Our focus at this symposium has been, as it should be, on the more formal library and information networks.

In preparing my remarks for this presentation I felt I needed to review where we were and where we are, before looking at where I think we will go from here.

We have already heard some of the impressive developments in the last fifteen years. In reviewing these developments we should keep in mind the parallel growth of two types of networks, which, for want of better terminology, are often referred to as library networks and information networks. Library networks were established to share cataloging and improve systems for interlibrary loan. Most of the records are at the monographic level. Information networks, such as Lockheed DIALOG, System Development Corporation and Bibliographic Retrieval Service, were developed to provide online access to information contained in abstracting and indexing services. Originally, most of the records were for journal articles, conference papers, and other documents at the analytic level. Of course, the information networks now include factual and numeric data, in addition to bibliographic records.

In his review of online library networking, Glyn Evans[3] identified seven conditions to be met before online networks could exist. These are (1) the development and use of online computing and the supporting telecommunications network; (2) the dramatic reduction in the unit cost of computing and telecommunications; (3) economic pressures and the labor-intensive nature of library and information

---

[1]*Information Technology: Critical Choices for Library Decision Makers*, ed. by Allen Kent and Thomas J. Galvin. New York, Marcel Dekker, Inc., 1982. p 151.

[2]Presentation at Western Information Network on Energy, 4 August 1981, Santa Fe, New Mexico

[3]*Bulletin of ASIS*, Volume 5, Number 5, 5 June 1979, p. 11.

services; (4) the "publishing" explosion; (5) the existence of standards, primarily technical and electronic, and especially the MARC (Machine-Readable Cataloging) formats; (6) changing modes of publication; and (7) society's need for broader and more timely sources of information and information access created by such pressures as environmental concerns and the delivery of medical care.

All of the conditions were met by the early 1970s. Perhaps the most critical bibliographic event for library network development was the creation of the MARC formats at the Library of Congress. The availability of catalog records in machine-readable form enabled Frederick Kilgour to turn a bright idea into reality, and OCLC went online in 1971. Other major library networks followed soon after with BALLOTS (now RLIN) in November 1972, UTLAS in December 1973 and WLN in 1975. In August 1971 there were *100,000* records online through OCLC. In 1971, Lockheed had fewer than five databases available online.

In little more than a decade, dramatic changes in the size of the files, the number of users, and the sophistication of both the systems and the users have taken place. Funding for these developments has come from the institutions participating, from state tax funds, private sector money, foundations, and from federal funds, particularly under the Library Services and Construction Act. As the networks and their use have changed, so have many of the issues.

The National Commission itself has long been active in the networking area. In the early to mid-1970s, soon after it was established, NCLIS commissioned several studies and issued a series of papers related to "A National Program for Library and Information Services." A major component of this program was "A Nationwide Network Concept." Since that time the Commission has supported, either separately or with other groups, studies of library photocopying, computer network protocol standards activities of ANSI Z39, and studies of the roles of various components, such as school library media programs, the Library of Congress, and government publications. Most recently, in cooperation with the Special Libraries Association (SLA), NCLIS has supported a Task Force on the Role of the Special Library in Networks and Cooperatives. The monumental report (some 272 pages plus appendices) of this excellent Task Force, which was chaired by Patricia Berger of the National Bureau of Standards, will be presented to the Commission at its April 1983 meeting. It contains thirteen specific recommendations to SLA and NCLIS.

TONI CARBO BEARMAN: "In my opinion, the Network Advisory Committee will continue to be one of the key groups in deciding 'Where From Here.' It is a group to take very seriously and to participate in actively. I have said that the issues have changed. We no longer (not that all of us *ever* did) think in terms of a *single* nationwide network."

In addition, NCLIS continues to work very closely with the Network Advisory Committee to the Library of Congress. This group has taken on increased significance, not only in its roles of advising the Librarian of Congress and providing input to the Council on Library Resources on the design and development of a nationwide network, but perhaps more importantly, as a principal focal point for nationwide network planning and policy. The Network Advisory Committee has expanded its membership to include:

> associations of organizations formally constituted and functioning in the public and private (for profit or not-for-profit) sector engaged in library and information services networking or network development, or having an impact on the development of a nationwide library and information services network and [that] can make a unique contribution to NAC.

Categories of membership have been defined, and now, in addition to associations, national libraries/federal information agencies, national bibliographic networks (such as OCLC, RLG/RLIN), the categories make specific distinctions between "regional/special bibliographic system operators" (such as AMIGOS, CLASS, SOLINET and WLN) and "network service organizations," such as BCR, MIDLNET, MINITEX, and NELINET, although the distinctions between these two categories are not as clear as they might be. In addition, a concerted effort is being made to include National Reference Systems, such as DIALOG Information Retrieval Service, Bibliographic Retrieval Service and System Development Corporation. The Institute for Scientific Information has become a member. Recent meetings of NAC have focused on document delivery and on the role of the public and private sectors.

In my opinion, the Network Advisory Committee will continue to be one of the key groups in deciding "Where From Here." It is a group to take very seriously and to participate in actively.

I have said that the issues have changed. We no longer (not that all of us *ever* did) think in terms of a *single* nationwide network. Also, the roles of many of the players have changed significantly. State and regional networks have re-examined their purposes and roles. Some have died, others have expanded. The next meeting of the Network Advisory Committee will focus on state networks.

I wish that Henriette Avram were at this symposium. She is one of the best-informed and most articulate spokespersons in this field.

TONI CARBO BEARMAN: "Networking has been called an 'unnatural' act. It requires cooperation, which Stella Keenan aptly defines as a lost of people cooing and a couple of people operating."

If you haven't read her excellent paper on "Network-level Decisions: Basic and Key Issues" from the 1981 Pittsburgh Conference on The Impact of Technology on Libraries, I urge you to do so. Henriette and I usually agree on most issues. This area is no exception. For many years, she has been saying that the problems and issues are not technical or technology; they are economic and political. I completely agree with her. Networking has been called an "unnatural" act. It requires cooperation, which Stella Keenan aptly defines as a lot of people cooing and a couple of people operating.

In her paper, Henriette summarized her view of the current scene. I would like to quote the five points of her summary:

> (1) LC as the major producer of bibliographic records through its MARC Distribution Service; (2) three bibliographic utilities, a) OCLC as the largest data resource and serving all types of libraries nationwide, b) RLIN as a utility specializing in services to a type of library, and c) WLN as a regional system for all types of libraries; (3) several projects, either operational or in the planning stage, designed to cooperatively build a data base and/or share records through a communications facility; (4) service centers, predominantly regional in their coverage, some planning or implementing computer-based systems of their own to serve their members; and (5) locally operated automated systems at individual libraries.

Given the above, it becomes obvious that the three utilities are not alike, and perhaps we ought to stop discussing them as though they were. RLIN and WLN are similar in that they serve a limited membership, one limited as to type of library and the other as to geographic area. In both cases, the limited membership appears to permit more complete library service. OCLC, on the other hand, is a major data resource, possibly taking on the aspect of a central node of a nationwide network. It is increasingly obvious that there is an impetus toward decentralization for the more regional requirements, in conjunction with a centralized data resource. Such distributed data processing has exciting possibilities.

The current situation for the information networks indicates continued competition among them, with DIALOG still in the lead as the "supermarket" provider of databases. There is a clear shift toward provision of customized and individualized services, which I have referred to as Era IV, following the three eras defined by Vin-

TONI CARBO BEARMAN: "Given the above [summary by Henriette Avram], it becomes obvious that the three utilities are not alike, and perhaps we ought to stop discussing them as though they were... It is increasingly obvious that there is an impetus toward decentralization for the more regional requirements, in conjunction with a centralized data resource."

cent Guiliano in "Into the Information Age." Many information networks are providing user aids, such as BRS' "After Dark" or DIALOG's "Knowledge Index" to assist home computer users in searching files. We are also seeing database providers, which formerly were "wholesalers" of their products, becoming retailers. Chemical Abstracts Service and Institute for Scientific Information are just two examples.

With these changing roles and developments for both library and information networks comes a revival of two key issue areas identified by Henriette Avram and discussed widely in the library/information community: ownership and governance. Some of the issues are:

1. Who owns a database compiled in part from information in the public domain and in part by participating members in a network? Who owns the individual records *within* the database? Who owns the records you or I enhance?
2. Who pays? Should the creator of records be compensated?
3. How can we best integrate other records, such as those describing archives, into networks? Also as Henriette has pointed out,
4. "A central facility as a data resource. . . may be the most efficient device. However, the designation of such a center raises the question as to whether there is any danger in the monopoly that would result. A monopoly can mean higher prices, non-responsiveness, and a lack of innovation." Should we have a central node or facility with regional nodes?
5. Who should govern networks and how should they be governed?

Other issues include:

6. What should the roles of state and regional networks be?
7. What role, if any, should the Federal government play? Who within the Federal government should be involved? We have come a long way from the view that the Federal government should provide all the answers and solutions and from the emphasis on any single centralized system.
8. How can we develop and improve links among library and information networks? *Should* these links be developed? How can we continue to improve document delivery?

96 *Library Networking: Current Problems and Future Prospects*

TONI CARBO BEARMAN: "A central facility as a data resource. . . may be the most efficient device. However, the designation of such a center raises the question as to whether there is any danger in the monopoly that would result. A monopoly can mean higher prices, non-responsiveness, and a lack of innovation."

9. At least one "national agency outside the U.S. has expressed unwillingness to have its data distributed by the Library of Congress to any U.S. organization that provides products and services to other institutions without the organization first negotiating a licensing agreement between itself and the national agency." (Avram paper, p. 166). Foreign governments are making decisions restricting or taxing the use of U.S. databases and services. Who should be involved in decisions concerning international networking agreements and international information policy issues?
10. Should we work to integrate library/information networks with local area networks? What, if any, should the relationship be?

These are only a few of the difficult and challenging issues confronting us. "Where From Here" is certainly first to understand these issues, to discuss them in meetings such as this, and to try to come up with some answers.

Second, we need to re-examine the appropriate roles of the various stakeholders in the public sector at all levels—federal, state and local—and in both the for-profit and not-for-profit components of the private sector. The Network Advisory Committee is the appropriate body to do this. We should strengthen our participation in the Committee, share the information from their meetings, and actively support their work.

Third, at the national level we will continue our assistance to Congress on the revision of LSCA and other library and information legislation to strengthen the resource sharing and networking components. It is important that all of you make your views heard on the legislation and on support for funding for LSCA programs as Congress decides on appropriations for LSCA.

Fourth, and last, continued discussion among the many stakeholders about the issues, problems, barriers and solutions is essential. This symposium is an excellent mechanism for that. In the words of the immortal "Cool Hand Luke" let us make sure that we do not "have here a failure to communicate." The economic and political issues, coupled with continued rapid technological developments, will continue to present major challenges in the next decade. Together, I am sure that we can rise to meet these challenges.

Thank you.

David Kaser

Thank you very much, Toni.

* * *

OK, we got twenty minutes. Let's be back in our chairs at three-twenty and have all those questions that you've been saving up ready to fire away at the panel. In twenty minutes. . .

Panel Discussion

David Kaser, Moderator

I think it's probably useful to remind ourselves whence we have come, lest we fall in the trap of thinking that there is something new under the library sun. There is not.

I thought it would be useful to review the first formal library network on this continent. As many of you perhaps know, this was conceptualized and established by the great English churchman, the Rev. Thomas Bray, who came to this continent as a commissary for the Anglican Church in 1696 and suffered culture shock when he got here because he found there weren't any books. He couldn't imagine how a culture could succeed without any books.

He went back to England and dedicated the balance of his life to getting books to the American continent and in 1701, wrote a book defining a library network for the British colonies in America. It was entitled *Bibliotheca Americanae Quadripartitae.*

What he conceptualized was a four-level library structure where every parish would have two libraries separated by subject; one for the clergy and the other for the laity. And then in every town, there would be a larger library. In every colonial capitol city, there would be a large library. These libraries would be indexed and the indexes exchanged so that the books themselves could also be exchanged.

That book was published in 1701. As I said, he dedicated the balance of his life to seeing that books were sent to America. He established two foundations to do this. Both of them you may have heard of. One was the Society for the Propagation of the Gospel in Foreign Parts. This was his creature, and its purpose was to get books to America. The second was the Society for the Promotion of Christian Knowledge. Even though these both sound like church organizations, that's because knowledge was church-oriented at that time, rather than because of any uni-dimensional intent that he had.

Before he [Thomas Bray] died in 1731, thirty-nine thousand volumes had been sent to the American colonies to establish this first

DAVID KASER: "I thought it would be useful to review the first formal library network on this continent. . . . this was conceptualized and established by. . . the Rev. Thomas Bray, who came to this continent as a commissary for the Anglican Church in 1696 and suffered culture shock when he got here because he found there weren't any books. . . . he went back to England and dedicated the balance of his life to getting books to the American continent and in 1701, wrote a book defining a library network for the British colonies in America.

library network. By 1740, they had all disappeared. So who knows, ten years from now, we may not have a library network on this continent and we have historical experience to indicate that; that may be the direction it's [networking] going.

Now, it's your turn. You've listened to my colleagues and myself through most of the day, but now you can "have at them." As I invited you to do earlier, I trust you've made notes of your questions, comments, observations, and concerns as they have been elicited by the presentations of our panelists.

Jim Edgar indicated before he left that although he would not be here to take questions orally, if you want to, you can write him a letter and he'd be glad to try to answer it by mail. He wasn't running and hiding. The rest of you may want to do the same thing.

Who has a question?

Question: This is directed to Laima Mockus of NELINET: Are you tied in with that New England preservation center?

Laima Mockus: I was asked if NELINET is tied into the New England NEDCC. No, we're not. In fact, I think they recently incorporated as an independent corporation.

Question: Are you doing any preservation or conservation work at all?

Mockus: No, we're not.

Question: My question is directed to Dr. Bearman. On international problems, how about UNESCO? Doesn't UNESCO have a role in this?

Toni Bearman: Yes, indeed it does. It is one of many organizations that does. UNESCO has what is called a General Information Program, which is a major program that cuts across disciplinary programs within UNESCO. There is a U.S. National Committee for UNESCO that is comprised of approximately twenty-five library and information associations here in this country. The Commission has just taken over responsibility of Secretariat for the National Committee. One of the reasons we have done so is that we feel that UNESCO could and should be playing a more active role in helping to resolve some of the library and information issues. We also were requested to do this by the State Department because they want additional expertise on what the U.S. position should be. In addition, we see that this will provide for us a forum with some of the best experts in the international field from the library/information com-

102   Library Networking: Current Problems and Future Prospects

DAVID KASER: "Before he [Thomas Bray] died in 1731, thirty-nine thousand volumes had been sent to the American colonies to establish this first library network. By 1740, they had all disappeared. So who knows, ten years from now, we may not have a library network on this continent and we have historical experience to indicate that; that may be the direction it's going."

munity. We plan to have the group get together frequently and also to set up a short newsletter to make sure we communicate information among all of ourselves and the associations, which we hope they will then pick up and put into their own association newsletter. That group will be meeting in May for the first time since we have taken over as Secretariat, and I think you will be seeing much more activity from that particular group. It's very sticky because UNESCO, of course, is a group of governments and different countries and I feel very strongly that anything in the library/information field has to have the three components participating at all times. The public sector, the not-for-profit sector and the for-profit sector, because those are the components that make up the library/information products and services and to not include any one of those groups would not be appropriate. The U.S. National Committee does have representation from the information industry, the archival community, the American Society for Information Science and the Association of American Publishers, in addition to the library and information associations, so we do hope to see UNESCO playing a more active role. But we also are working with other associations, such as IFLA (the International Federation of Library Associations), the International Council of Scientific Unions Abstracting Board (called ICSUAB), and other international groups. It is just such a complicated area. It's also, within the U.S. Government, difficult to know where to turn. The State Department is involved, the Department of Commerce, Executive Office of the President, Congress itself, Government Printing Office, the three national libraries. It's taken a long time just to find out who the key players are and most of them have changed within the last couple of months.

Rowland Brown: I'd like to add this dimension. I think Toni has very quickly described all of the complexities and I would suggest that perhaps if we're hoping for truly an international solution which all those three entities have agreed upon, none of us in this room will be around to enjoy in the terms of time. We have had enough problems just dealing with one entity, the British Library, over the last couple of years. It is a very poor profit-conscious organization we find as Henriette Avram has also found. As a result of lengthy negotiations (which after we had negotiated a settlement blew apart because they decided to go into developing an online system in the UK to be mounted in a couple of years), they decided that they would not make their UK MARC available to us unless we promised not to make it available to British libraries but only to U.S. libraries,

ROWLAND BROWN: "If you wait, if you don't take the initiative, I'm concerned that any kind of development of an international bibliographic and information network will never come about. We are working very actively in that area."

which I found rather interesting for a tax supported British institution. And we are simply taking our own individual action in the UK to, in effect, develop an alternative. That's the best way I would like to describe it. We're also discussing similar opportunities with entities in Western Europe and in South America because I think, in the long run, initiatives have to be taken which then all of those other international organizations and associations can react to. If you wait, if you don't take the initiative, I'm concerned that any kind of development of an international bibliographic and information network will never come about. We are working very actively in that area.

Bearman: Thanks for adding that particular point. UNESCO, I just wanted to add, is talking about developing a global network, which we find interesting since we have trouble developing one within a much smaller community in the U.S. I completely agree with what Rowland said. I feel that the broad international fora are very, very important so that we can share information about what is happening in bilateral agreements or between one country and one company or whatever these many, many different agreements are. One certainly doesn't preclude the other. We are going to be talking about the issues and problems for, I'm sure, hundreds of years to come, but I think we do need both the individual initiatives and the international fora such as the UNESCO group. I think that also raises another important point. Many times people say, "why don't we have a national information policy?" England does. Japan does. I think that many people don't understand how different each of those countries is. They may have a written policy that's quite different from what's in effect. Russia certainly has a national information policy that I would never like to see in this country. I think that we don't understand, in many cases, the differences between our countries. England, where we lived for four years, is very, very very different from this country, not only in that we're separated by the common language, but it does have a very different idea of what the federal government does. It supports private companies to come to trade shows, like the Special Libraries Association here in this country. It funds private sector companies. It controls not only the postal service and the telephone but the telegraph system. The role of the PTT in the different European countries makes very different authority and power, I think over networks than what we have in this Country. Ma Bell does not yet tell all of our networks (never will) what to do. Where PTT in a European country can actually tax data bases from outside the country, can do all sorts of things, because it's part of the government actually. So without going into lots of details, I think it is important that we all continue to educate ourselves about some of these differences and go to some of these international meetings. When IFLA is in New York in 1985, for example, I think everyone should make a real effort to get there to talk with some people from the different countries.

Question: Well, I was just thinking that here we get into the whole business of national security. We're concerned now about electronic information being stolen. I would imagine the government is even beginning to talk about international information systems and questioning them. Has that come up for discussion?

Bearman: It's not fair for me to answer all the questions, but they'll have to just kick me under the table to get me not to. The government has been discussing those questions since probably about 1776. Seriously, the first amendment to the Constitution is a very, very important amendment that relates exactly to those kinds of issues and I think that's one that we must not forget. There is no question that within the current administration, there's increased discussion of the need to protect the national security and how that may conflict with the need to disseminate, or the tradition of disseminating, scientific and technical information outside the U.S. There are many, many instances in the past couple of years when people have been denied access to information at meetings, have been kept from attending certain meetings because they are not U.S. citizens, not only because the information might endanger the national security but because there seems to be a concern that some countries might get a technological "leg up" on us more than some already have. So information is being seen, not just as a resource, but as a valuable commodity to be traded around which I think personally is a real mistake. To have that kind of limit is an error, in my personal opinion. I'm going to get struck by a bolt from heaven, I'm sure, but that's why I work for an independent agency that advises both the administration and Congress. It's not that simple, though. Clearly there are certain instances where we don't want to give away information that might endanger someone's life. We do not in any way wish to give away private information about individuals. It's essential that we protect certain kinds of information. We should never talk about information in the abstract. I think we have to define whether we're talking about personal information, corporate, proprietary, information products, information services, and then

TONI CARBO BEARMAN: "We should never talk about information in the abstract. I think we have to define whether we're talking about personal information, corporate, proprietary, information products, information services, and then set the limits and develop many, many policies for the different kinds of information and the different circumstances."

set the limits and develop many, many policies for the different kinds of information and the different circumstances. There's a lot of discussion of that going on. Questions of reciprocity: are we giving away more than we're getting? It's been a topic that the Commission has been focusing on. At our last meeting, we had two experts come and talk with us. At our meeting next week, we're having someone from the Department of Defense come and give us a slightly different view, to try to educate us about what some of these very, very complicated issues are. I think the more you get into them, the worse it turns out to be a Pandora's box.

Question: This you don't have to answer, Toni. I've heard today two speakers talk in two different directions. I think I would like to clarify that a little bit about who the customer of the networks is? NELINET seems to think their customers are libraries, and someone else said something about being concerned directly with patrons. I have some questions about that in terms of marketing strategy. It seems to me that the network is an entrepreneurial animal, and so marketing has to be a part of the operating plan. The undertone that I seem to be hearing today is that we want to be doing marketing studies, not of the libraries that we serve but of the patrons who end up using them. I'd like to know if that's true and if it is true how it will be implemented?

Mockus: NELINET sees itself as an intermediary, a facilitator, a supporter of a library achieving its own goals. So it is up to the library to deal with its own community and its own patrons. Our focus is therefore providing the most services. We market to the library. We market by attending six state library associations annually, plus the New England Library Conference, exhibiting. We have open houses for multitype libraries once a month in the office. We conduct and hold demonstrations, not just of OCLC, we also broker three information-retrieval data bases. But we also conduct open houses to demonstrate electronic mail systems, new printers, etc. There are two thousand terminals that you can conceivably use to connect to any information utility, and whenever we come across one that is reasonable, seems to work well, we demonstrate it also. Our role is not to tell any of our two hundred and sixty member libraries that they should choose this one over the other. Our role is to centrally demonstrate to them what is available and let them evaluate and judge for themselves whether a particular product will enable them to serve their clientele more easily. It's difficult when you are serving multitype libraries, very large and very small ones;

LAIMA MOCKUS: "Our focus is therefore providing the most services. We market to the library."

therefore, we focus much more on supporting the library, the library staff and the library administration to select and utilize whatever fits within their own planning in providing services for their community. Now, Rowland, you can contradict it all.

Brown: Let me just supplement it. I think I made a comment in my talk someplace about distinguishing governing and marketing. First of all, we have contracts for OCLC services with each of some twenty-some-odd networks. The official organization with whom we deal, by contract, by obligation, who is responsible to carry out their obligations and functions to us, are the networks. The networks in turn are required, by OCLC and by their own boards in terms of other things they may be doing (because not all of them are only handling OCLC service; in fact, state and federal networks are obviously chartered for many other public purpose functions), to have contracts with individual libraries. These obligate the libraries to carry out certain obligations with respect to cataloging and system use in terms of paying for those services and so forth. However, what I'm suggesting is that the networks in the libraries are ultimately, all of us, serving the patrons of libraries, whether those patrons are faculties of universities and colleges, whether they're students, whether they are the general public, in terms of public libraries, whether they are federal employees or state employees. If any of us do not think through what is the ultimate user of that information, we do so at our peril. What I'm suggesting is that in designing systems and in thinking of how systems are going to be used in the future, particularly as we talk about distribution and local options, personal computers, use of commercial or for-profit information alternatives to those that are available within universities, colleges, public libraries and so forth, we have to understand that person out there in terms of what they want, how they want it, and how they're going to access it. What are they willing to support in the future, by taxes, by tuition, by fees, by whatever? No information is free. It may be freely accessible by public law, for public policy purposes. That only means that the public has decided to make it available and accessible freely. But in terms of the economics somebody has to put it in the form that they can access; otherwise it becomes a mirage in terms of you have access to information but you have no economics if they're not there to get it. One of the things that quite honestly concerns me, and I'm sure Toni and everybody else on this panel, is that I see the future where a greater part of our public is going to be disenfranchised, not only by eco-

ROWLAND BROWN: "If any of us do not think through what is the ultimate user of that information, we do so at our peril. . . . One of the things that quite honestly concerns me. . . is that I see the future where a greater part of our public is going to be disenfranchised, not only by economics and job opportunities, but informationally."

nomics and job opportunities, but informationally. I am concerned that the information society is not going to be the millenium in which everybody has equal access to information from an economic standpoint, in fact, the barriers are going to be wider. That needs to be a very significant concern of all of us unless we really economically, politically, and socially disenfranchise a large portion of our public. That's a long-winded way of saying, yes, OCLC is very interested in the ultimate user wherever they are and in fact our mission objective approved by our Board and user's council and which appears in our annual report, so states.

Frank Grisham: Could I add just a bit to that? I think Rowland has accurately reflected my position on it. What I tried to say in my presentation was that we should avoid the self-serving posture that we accidentally fall into sometime because we do not know exactly how to interpret the need in the libraries as they try to relate to the patron. I know, I can give you examples of where we've developed programs that have had little effect on the patron. I think every time our Boards in our networks act, they should ask the question, "what effect does this have on the patron?" The responsibility of interpretation is where I think we are weak. I mean, the art of interpretation. The libraries, the staffs, the administration of the libraries. If they are properly representing the needs of the patron, then that's the source, that's the important source. But as a former library director, I feel we were particularly inadequate in this area and particularly inadequate in reflecting the needs of the patron. On up the pipeline, so to speak, to the networks and to the utilities. I believe that pretty well covers it. If we can get the library staffs to interpret the needs of the patrons effectively then I would feel much more comfortable.

Kaser: I think things must have gone to pot at Vanderbilt after I left, Frank. I'm sorry to hear that.

Question: This Conference opened this morning with an address from our State Librarian who also happens to be Secretary of State, Mr. Edgar, who's a very articulate spokesman for our network and our needs. It also happens that he and the library community in this State are searching for a new state library director who serves under the state librarian. Frank Grisham answered the question that Toni posed later on behalf of NAC. NAC has coming on its next agenda the role of the states in library networking. Frank tells us that there is and there will be a future for states in networking. He wasn't sure about the multistate groups because they didn't have that constituency in the boundaries that support them. I wonder if our guest here in

Illinois from the networks in Indiana, New England, SOLINET might want to bring it down very sharply and focus for us into terms that they think Illinois should be looking for in its next library director. In terms of the agenda for states as they play a role in networking, we've heard from McCoy, Brown, and some others suggesting that there are some revolutions going around having to do with microcomputers, etc. and I know that there are some concerns in some of these regional networks about where their future's going to be. So I invite some advice from the panelists.

Barbara Markuson: I think the state library position has traditionally been a very strange one. It was expressed recently, in something I read, as responsibility without authority. That's a very difficult thing, in a sense, to be held accountable for something as complex as the library service in a State. What does that really mean? I think most of us know that it doesn't mean that we can go out, naturally, and administer libraries, or change how libraries operate. We have to use certain kinds of leadership and persuasion and I think another anomaly comes about because that is the traditional way we get grant money and then one has the responsibility of leadership through the use of money as a catalyst. I think the most appropriate role is to facilitate and to be concerned ultimately with the user. If you concentrate on the user, then you can bypass some of the political issues, I think, of looking at what certain libraries are doing. I think much of the arguments we do in libraries can be settled very readily if we go to more meetings with more data. Are we, in fact, improving? What kind of users should we be serving? On the issue of control, I personally think that the Indiana model, where the network is governed by the members but still has a state accountability, has certain benefits because it protects the members from risk. I think networks can more readily accept risk. Organizations like state universities, state libraries need to always be able to have the confidence of the legislators. I think that money coming in is very important, in some cases then it becomes very difficult to take risks or unpopular projects or problems. I think that the network can, as an independent agency, handle some of those kind of things. So the best situation of all is someone who is very interested in technology, extremely concerned for the user, very able to move a community forward and to create the climate for addressing difficult issues and facilitate and then in a sense say "ok, you people go on with it."

Mockus: I agree with everything that Barbara said but I probably would add a couple of other things. I would say that a State Library Director should be very aware of what is available and what has been done, should be able to direct and focus internal funds, be very politically astute, should realize that networking in the past ten years has moved us all beyond state lines and boundaries. This is not a time to go back and refocus in a very narrow way as to what a richer state, a more powerful state might be able to do for its own internal network. The person should be very comfortable with the idea that "not invented here" is ok. We can still utilize it for our own statewide patrons, and not waste energy duplicating what is available elsewhere. I think that a State Library Director, say in ILLINET, probably could focus the state's energies on perhaps using some of the new technology, such as microwave connections that simply enhance what the kind of networking that is already available. Most of all, like the rest of us, it should be someone who can walk on water.

Kaser: That's what I was thinking—Jesus Christ for $21,000 a year.

Mockus: $19,000!

Bearman: May I add a comment to that? I particularly don't want the ordinary citizen who merely walks on water. I work with many people through the COSLA group and I find that it requires apparently a lot of political astuteness, the ability to communicate, a good sense of judgment. Certainly some of them have other wonderful qualities, such as a good voice to sing in a barbershop quartet, some are wonderful dancers; it does require that sense of humor and I think probably, instead of just someone walking on water, first your new director should turn it into wine and then walk on it.

Question: I understood you to say earlier that there were pros and cons to a single state network. I think I heard you say the pros but I think you teased us. I would like to hear some of the cons. Particularly in light of the Simon proposal and amendment for LSCA which has a wonderful emphasis on networking and cooperation, but a teaser I guess if you will about how those funds might be distributed and I can see that there are a lot of different networks that have a lot of different ideas about how they might get some of that money when that legislation is approved.

Markuson: I left my notes in my briefcase, so I'll try to reconstitute what I think some of the disadvantages are. Let me say that I was talking about the kind of network that we represent. So, if we were in the SOLINET area or could draw upon a network such as

SOLINET, how should we have organized in Indiana? I think that's the question you're asking? I'll just try to put it in that context. One of the things that I think we lack continuously is the ability to fund more technical expertise that's devoted solely to the network, not the borrowing, the occasional academic expert, or having the occasional consultant. I think we need the range of skills that requires a fairly expensive staff and I think that proper funding is probably on the order of $300 to $400 thousand dollars a year to do a job well, so one of the things that makes it more difficult if the State is smaller is that network staff then proceed to be a lot of fat cats. There is a kind of relationship of how much we are able to fund so I see that as one of the disadvantages. The other disadvantage comes where members have very unique needs. You may not have enough of them in the State to be able to give them that kind of attention. We've done some joint things for example with Illinois in the area like map cataloging or manuscript cataloging. You don't have a lot of people and we don't have a lot of people, so how do we meet those more specialized needs? So I think it was disadvantages like that I was thinking of. So, if we could draw on a SOLINET, our program could be addressed much more to spending more time working with the library and we would then rely on them for a lot of the technical developments. In fact, we do contract with SOLINET to do some things that we can't afford to do. On balance, I don't see any prospect of us getting a regional network. I think we've been through that, though perhaps there is an opportunity for the networks in the midwest to work together a little bit more closely than we have on some of these other issues.

Question: I have one message, two comments and one question. First of all, I would like to show my appreciation to all the excellent speakers for your very informative and inspiring speeches which have helped me personally and I think I'll convey to my colleagues at home of your experiences in building a network. I would like to thank you all for your excellent presentations, and for the excellent preparation and the organization of this Symposium. As from what I've said, you may know I'm from Taiwan, Republic of China, and regarding the complicated issue of international cooperation or international networking, Dr. Bearman and Dr. McCoy mentioned something in that respect and Dr. Brown also said something about it. It's a matter of mutual respect and mutual willingness to help one another. Like RLG people and the Chinese Library and library automation community have helped one another very well, and the RLG group has also adopted use of the Chinese character set as their main frame to build up their characters of Chinese titles. So, it's up to each nation to be able to get away from the politics and to cooperate on an equal standing. What I am concerned about is that politics do get into these things. Like Montreal IFLA meeting. We had seventeen registrations, everything was paid, but no visa was issued. People were waiting outside, in the U.S., for visas from Canada, for ten days, until the Conference was over, the delegates never got in. So there wouldn't be any way to communicate, or to cooperate if such meetings can not be participated in because of some political issues. So these international organizations like IFLA and UNESCO should be completely non-governmental. And that's my request. I hope that Dr. Bearman, in the future, you will try to see to it that most of the conferences even with different political standing—they can go and share their opinions. My question is about networking. I think I heard the pros and cons about centralized networking and the decentralized way of the grassroots way, about top down, bottom up. So in a small place, an island like ours, what do you suggest would be the best way, grassroots up or top down? I think it has something to do with the government's organization as a whole. I don't know if that's true or not. I'd like your advice on that.

Kaser: That's a good question! I don't know whether any of the panelists are going to want to take that on. We do have a situation in this country, don't we, where the responsibility for education and related issues is farmed out to the fifty states by virtue of our Constitution. Not all countries are structured like that. Does that have an impact?

Brown: I think there is a cultural issue here. I think all of our speakers today, and the people we have quoted from magazines and books as well, have pointed out that in the United States, we have a strong tendency when left to our own devices to "centricate." We go out and we start from the grassroots up. We are typically wary or leery of any kind of centralized operation. Not all cultures are that way. Many cultures feel very much more comfortable with something that is coming down in a sense that they've all agreed upon, whether it be a Japanese culture, some other European cultures. I don't think we should say how it should be done in Taiwan in that sense. I think it's what works and what people are comfortable with rather than a model in United States. I don't think the United States is necessarily a model for any other society when it comes to how we should work in a political structure. Let me give you an example. You raised the issue of Asian language services and RLG's activities and their special terminals. I think maybe that's a case in point. OCLC had a small grant from the National Endowment for Humanities to work in this field. I looked at what we were receiving from the National Endowment which was something like ninety thousand dollars and I looked at the program that would eventually be required to implement it, the cost of the terminals that would eventually be used and determined we would be imposing on our general membership close to a million dollar development. And terminals which are very expensive. For, at this point in time, a relatively few in the totality of users. The only way that could reasonably be funded are two ways: either on a national grant of some kind or a foundation grant. Certainly not by transaction fees which is the typical way we have had to finance our development within OCLC. RLG, in turn, did receive grants and is going ahead with them but those grants have come from foundations. Now if you have foundations that are willing to do that on a national basis for everyone then you do not have to have central government support for it, but that's in a form of a tax supported function because those foundations are tax free organizations that have collected those funds for those purposes or the federal government can do it. Again, I think it's a question of how it is most appropriate to be done in a particular country, but that's the reason OCLC did not proceed. We expect as time goes by for our libraries and OCLC to participate in that program on a cost effective basis, because basically tax supported funds have been used for the development.

Bearman: First of all, thank you very much for your comments. We do appreciate that. A lot of work goes into preparing a talk for one of these and it's very nice to know that it was listened to carefully and appreciated. Thank you. I will make certain that as part of our role in advising the State Department, we convey your comments back to them. I am horrified to learn that I am only somewhat grateful it was not the U.S. that did that, but Canada. Although that does not make us any better but I will certainly make sure that we take those comments back. That is a terrible thing to hear about. In terms of what you should do, I think it would be ridicuously presumptous for me to sit here, never having visited your Country and tell you what you should do. I can make suggestions 1) to make sure you have a careful planning effort that involves those who will be involved in using any networking system that you have, the ultimate users as well as the library and information community. Another obvious part which we, I think, are learning from our mistakes, is the importance of including the many different components as we see more and more executive work stations in industry, or work stations for the researchers within our universities. We see how important the integration of the local area networks, the use of home computers is, to any kind of network to be developed. Of course tying in with that, the need to deliver the documents that people need so that we don't frustrate them by quickly providing a list of twenty documents, only three of which are available. So perhaps you can learn some from the mistakes that we have all made in our past few years of networking and some of the things I think we have done very well. I think the U.S. has certainly taken a leadership role in some of the best networks in the world. Beyond that, I would be happy to help provide information about what we know is available but I certainly would not want to recommend to you what you should be doing. I don't know anywhere near enough about your country to make a suggestion.

Markuson: I have one more thing to add: Find someone close in the U.S. that you can call on a regular basis. I have a friend who is working in technology network planning in Australia and she calls me regularly to check to find out if what the vendors are telling her when they get to Australia that they have just been purchased in every library in the U.S. We check out some of those things.

Kaser: I remember back in 1972 when the IFLA meeting was held in Budapest and the South Korean delegation cooled its heels in Vienna throughout the entirety of the Conference because it was unable to get visas to go into Hungary. At that time I shrugged and said "Well, it's Hungary," and then when I see the same thing happening to delegations trying to get into Canada, that's a little closer home. I realize that it's a sovereign country over which we have no control at all, but I hope this never happens in our Country.

Question: The RLG microfilming preservation program—I'd like to know whether or not you could talk a little bit more about how it's determined. What form it's taking, how decisions are made and how it relates to activities going on in LC?

Richard McCoy: One of the things I would like to tell you is that we feel very pleased right at this time because we've just been the recipients of two relatively large grants. One of them from the Mellon Foundation and the other from NEH, each of six hundred seventy-five thousand dollars that will help us to support that particular activity. The project activity will go on among those member institutions who have decided in particular to take part and not necessarily all our RLG members. The decisions will be made in common and jointly, records will be maintained in RLIN so that we know which microfilming is going on and who's doing it. It will be those participating members who are making those particular decisions. There are some aspects of the program that we're working on very vigorously at the moment. For instance, we will be providing the common storage location for archival microfilm storage. As it appears now, it is likely to be in a cave in Pennsylvania. We sent some of our staff out on a spelunking expedition a while back. We will be storing material there for true archival purposes in which we don't expect them to be service masters from which copies are made, but genuine archival backup, and the amount of activity there should be small. I'm not really in a position to comment on the relationship that this will have to similar activity at LC. I think it is our desire and we hope it is their's that we want to operate in such a way that we're not unnecessarily duplicating activity and filming. Filming is terribly expensive and I think it's expensive enough so that there are tremendous economic pressures on us to be sure that we don't do that work redundantly.

Question: There are more have-nots in the world than people outside the United States. In Illinois, there are many small libraries who do not have access to the technology which you people offer. Barbara Markuson talked a little bit about what the challenges are to be met by the smaller libraries. What I would like to know is what are your plans to provide access to your kinds of services to smaller libraries than you're currently offering or if you consider that to be a part of your challenge?

Markuson: I think the one point I'd like to get across is that I consider that we have an obligation to look at small libraries, and to be concerned about small libraries, without being sentimental about small libraries. In other words, the technology that we could provide them still has to fit within their budget. We're not in a position to offer free technology to any class of libraries, so one of the things we would be concerned to do is that services that we put up in the State are offered in such a way that there is some equity or some arrangement. For example, we're looking at the possibility of shared circulation clusters. I know you have a similar development in this State and trying to look at cost arrangements that I think would make those very attractive networks for that type of library. They could

BARBARA MARKUSON: "I consider that we have an obligation to look at small libraries, and to be concerned about small libraries, without being sentimental about small libraries."

get into that kind of an arrangement for initial cost of around ten thousand dollars and ongoing costs of around five to six thousand a year, which makes that affordable to a whole class of libraries that couldn't reach OCLC. I think we have to remember that a lot of small libraries do get an indirect benefit now because through our resource sharing networks, much of the material that gets into their hands is identified and located and requested for through the OCLC data base, so they're getting that indirect benefit. The other possibility is as I mentioned. As we find technology that might be appropriate, we seek grants or work with the utilities to see how it can interface and apply. I don't think the vendors are going to do that for us. I think we have to do that. We would be continually concerned about that and in fact would be looking to see if we could find vendors that would be interested in looking at really low-cost technology for in-state network access.

Brown: I think one of the major concerns that OCLC has is that while as I mentioned earlier, some six thousand libraries are accessing OCLC one way or another, still in terms of the total libraries out there, that's still a relatively small number. Statistically, I think those libraries serve the majority of the population of the United States if you want to look at it that way, but nevertheless, many, many, small libraries today under the present structure of OCLC, present structure of RLG, WLN, and indeed any of the major computer networks (I hate the term, utilities, I just don't use it) are not in their present form able to serve those libraries. We're looking at various methods, the latest of which is what we refer to as group, an ILL group access where one library basically is an OCLC member and is the OCLC member that assumes the obligations of an OCLC member but other libraries affiliated with that group would be in a resource sharing cluster with that institution and thereby indirectly, in a sense, have access to OCLC at least for purposes of ILL. In some states, for instance in Michigan, New York, two states, through service bureaus, service centers, we have at least five or six hundred public libraries in those states accessing OCLC on a regular structured basis where as in some other states only a handful of libraries do and that's simply the way in which they have chosen to structure themselves to access networks. I think the use in the future of personal computers will enable small libraries to do a number of functions on that one terminal rather than just exclusively connecting with WLN or OCLC. You will open up avenues. I think that one of the major functions in the future of state networks is not to try to restructure a whole relationship that ignores what already exists in terms of working networks of larger universities, colleges, larger public libraries that already work reasonably well but somehow to bring in the smaller public libraries and school libraries in a way that builds upon and integrates with what is already available. I think this is an area that OCLC with all of our networks wants to work very closely on. In fact, we are staffing a position to be concerned just about this and nothing else. We were one of the people who urged the Council on Library Resources and NAC to take this under advisement as a major project. I think it's the single most important thing in networking in the immediate future for an institution like OCLC.

Bearman: I think this is a terribly important question. One of the areas we tend to forget is the many, many small libraries in this Country. We often focus on the large New York Publics, the major research libraries and others. I just recently put together an issue paper on libraries for a volume of issues that's going out to governors, mayors and other people around the Country. In putting that together, I used some of the statistics that Don Sager compiled in a study that he did under OCLC sponsorship, I might add, and I was absolutely astonished to find out that more than 64% of the libraries serve a population of fewer than ten thousand people. If there is such a thing as a typical public library (these are public libraries) this library serves fewer than ten thousand people, has a circulation of thirty thousand or fewer annually, a collection of fewer than forty thousand books, an annual budget of less than fifty thousand dollars. When you look at the hard facts, there are not ten thousand dollars a year to be spending on participating in networks so I think it is absolutely essential that we not lose track of the smaller libraries. There are still many libraries in this Country that do not yet have telephones. That is something that is easy to overlook because we do think that 97% of the population does have access to a library but that may mean you have to go two hundred miles to get to it or it may mean a bookmobile. It is terribly important that we not widen that gap between the information rich and the information poor, and the technology, Rowland was saying earlier, is likely to continue to widen that gap.

Question: I'd like to go back to the discussion that pointed to central planning for the development of regional and state networks at the national level. As our speakers made their presentations, it seemed that they took varying views on the importance of that in de-

TONI CARBO BEARMAN: "It is terribly important that we not widen that gap between the information rich and the information poor."

termining what the role of these networks will be and the kind of technological development that ought to occur. It seems to me that Frank Grisham was on the side furthest away from central or national planning. I thought it was interesting that Dr. Bearman indicated that in the last decade that they've made tremendous strides in the development of networking in a time when there was a distinct absence of national planning. So perhaps, Mr. Grisham, you could speak to or expand a bit on your position and perhaps some of the others could react to your comment.

Grisham: I think this is a fascinating question as to the need. The need is there for national planning, but I think that, given the circumstances of our history, that planning can play only a coordinating role. We do not have the structure at the moment. We do the planning to superimpose on the country the implementation. The money's not there, the structure's not there and we know the relationship of our local governments to the state governments, to the national government. The problems that are created with national planning in other areas beyond the library world and the lack of success in much of that. I think that the technology is moving so rapidly that it's causing the planning to be more profitable at the local level and at the state level where those entities at least have the political structure to implement that after the planning. There's a lot of planning that goes on that never reaches realization, good planning that just goes away and into the trash can or the files. That happens in your local library, your local government, state government. I believe that the natural evolvement as we cooperate and work together (that's planning) is going to result in a better structure than superimposing from on high. I think it's impossible for Toni or any of the other national agencies to do something that we'll all agree to. I think their coordinating role is important but that's about as far as it can possibly go.

Bearman: Thank you. That's a nice way to take me off the hook. Do we ever really want a single national plan? Is it ever feasible? It's not just recently, it's for at least two hundred years that we have developed a structure that gives certain powers to state government. Retain those powers, the States' Rights people would argue. It's a question that they did not wish to give those away. The funding for our public libraries, 95% of that comes from the state and local government. Where the money is, is also the power and the authority. They are not about to say "well, fine, we're going to give up all that and you sit in Washington and tell us what we should do here in

FRANK GRISHAM: "I think that the technology is moving so rapidly that it's causing the planning to be more profitable at the local level and at the state level where those entities at least have the political structure to implement that after the planning."

Montana." The other thing is that I don't think there is any single plan or system that is appropriate for all states or all communities, just as there is not one that would be appropriate for all different countries. Since I've been in my job, I've had the opportunity to travel considerably, one hundred days a year it comes out. I have visited New York Public Library, I visited a wonderful school library in a town that had a population of one hundred twenty-four people, I've been in rural areas smaller than the one I grew up in, in Connecticut. I've seen areas where you *do* have to go two hundred miles to get to a library. This is a very diverse country, thank God, and I hope it always remains that way. I just think it would be a mistake to try to come up with one solution that would be appropriate for everyone, even if we all were to agree to it. In addition, we do have other factors, a strong private sector, for-profit and not-for-profit. The American Library Association, a strong not-for-profit group, certainly has some views about what should be done in the networking area. Each state librarian does. Research communities would not wish to relinquish that authority or decision-making power to some group sitting in Washington, and if a plan were decided today, tomorrow might be different. It might be a different administration with a whole different approach to what should be done. This may sound strange for someone who works for the Federal Government but my feeling is I work for something like two hundred twenty-five million people. Living in London two years ago, I used to get asked what do the Americans think about such and such and I would want to say, well, speaking for two hundred twenty-five million people—so you realize in some ways how silly it is to try to come up with a single plan or program for anything to affect that many people, from that many different cultures, different backgrounds and different communities in fifty different states. And how about our non-contiguous states and territories? Very different kinds of questions and concerns there, too. I don't think it is a desirable thing to have a single plan. I know I may again be struck by a bolt of lightning from above but I think the times have changed considerably, and that there are not many who think that we should have one any longer if we ever should have in the first place.

McCoy: I would like to say that there is another national role which has been extremely essential to the kind of progress that has been made, the national cooperatively developed standards which are in place today. Without them, I think it would have been impossible for the networking progress that we've been disussing here to take place. When you think over the complexity of those standards and the kinds of participation that was necessary to bring them into being, it's an absolutely remarkable thing to me that it has happened at all. That's a national role that needs to be supported and nurtured and maintained by us all because it's essential to the next step also.

Markuson: I wanted to follow up on that point that perhaps we don't really mean to use the word "plan," but more that what we would like to have happen at the national level is to advance us forward in our concepts and to define certain issues. I was going to use the example of the MARC. LC looked out and saw bibliographic chaos because, and I was at LC at that time, we did a survey—fourteen million records had been converted into thirty-nine formats, none of them interchangeable. We had the will and the energy and the money, so in that sense that was a kind of national planning, but it was focused on a separate issue and it had tremendous impact. I think we went back to those days where somebody issued and showed us the hierarchy and how things fit together. What I would like to see now and encourage Toni to do, as she is able, as they focus in on the issues that we can then fold into our planning concepts because we don't always have the broadest view at the state level. We can't duplicate what they're doing at the national level. They see the issues in a different context than we do, so technology monitoring, identifying these issues and getting us concept and issues papers, I think would help advance the planning.

Bearman: I think that's terribly important and in no way am I saying there should not be a strong national role because I think there is a very, very important one. I guess my feeling is, I'm just concerned about trying to develop a single system, that kind of thing always bothers me. The idea of coordinating, of getting people together, providing the form and the catalyst, those are all extremely important. If you look at some of the work that the commission has done in its twelve years (ten before I got there, so I can take no credit for it) there would have been no computer-to-computer protocol work with the National Bureau of Standards, much of the work with the Library of Congress, very strong support for NSC Z39 over the years. The ability to step back and take a look and bring together task forces to look at such things as the role of special libraries in networking or the role of school media centers and then to share that information. What we are trying to do now and I think actually being very successful at it, is bring the library information community itself much more closely together. I think we're hearing a lot less of those publishers, those librarians, those whatever, it is much more of a forum which we do frequently, for example, having a monthly meeting of the key legislative people in all the library information associations, very informal, over coffee, but it works a lot. A lot can get done when somebody from IIA (Information Industry Association) sits down and talks with someone from the American Library Association in a non-threatening environment. I think what also is very important is that we've been working very closely with the state librarians. The COSLA (Chief Officers of State Library Agencies) group and the commission have a formal liaison with people attending both of the meetings. We've developed it to such a good point that we will be meeting together next week and having a dinner together and such with all of the state librarians and the members of the commission. We've also been scheduling our meetings at meetings of different associations so that our commissioners can get to know more about what is happening, at Special Libraries, at the Information Industry Association. I think that broadening of the means of communications has helped a lot, certainly in the role of standards, in providing the forum, in being that catalyst to make things happen. With our whopping budget of six hundred seventy-four thousand dollars, we don't put millions into research, but by bringing together a group of people or putting five thousand a year into NSC Z39, we can have a real impact by serving as a catalyst. Those are critical roles and I'm very much in favor of continuing and strengthening those.

McCoy: I'd like to follow up with an illustration, if I can, in the standards area that some of you may have a particular interest in. RLG has an interesting working relationship going on with the Getty Trust and the Getty Museum. One of the things that it has helped to underscore for us is the lack of a standard (like a MARC standard) for the description of works of art. We're in that situation that Barbara described of having lots and lots of material all over the country that has been cataloged in a variety of different schemes and no way to bring it together. That's a process that we'll be working on actively and the Getty people are very interested to have that happen and would like to have it happen in a great hurry. I'm worried about that a little bit because these are rather difficult things. As I left them ten days ago on the topic, I tried to warn them that they have the possibility of being in the world of standards somewhat like IBM is in standards for data processing. Because of their vast resources and energy they might well develop a standard which is their own and independent of what is accepted nationally. IBM has a corporate reason and purpose for doing that. I think neither the Getty nor RLG nor those of you here would share that kind of purpose.

Kaser: The problem is that the art field never had a Melvil Dewey.

Question: This is directed to Mr. McCoy. Since you're with RLG network and you seem to be interested in preservation on film and otherwise, I'm sure you're familiar with the fact that the Library of Congress is interested in the mass deacidification of paper and using diethylene gas or vapor under pressure. I was wondering if you had any plans to collaborate with them on this like getting a vacuum chamber and so on?

McCoy: We have no specific plans. We've worked with them in the preservation effort for a long time. We're aware of their progress and have looked at the result and are very pleased that it's there, our member institutions are. We hope that it will become less expensive and more widely available. It looks like a rather expensive process now. There are a series of new technologies that will be very exciting for preservation, some which are not to preserve the original material. I think in general, the problem that's being addressed there is with a particular range of materials that have that particular paper problem but there are a variety of other things that are happening that we are looking at very closely, and one of them is optical disks. In time, it has a great potential of being used as a replacement for microfilming and there are a number of things happening right now. In fact, in this area ITT has an interesting project which involves scanning of paper material, reformating it without the need to code the characters. It does it simply by the black spaces and the white spaces on the page, formatting into frames which are suitable for video encoding at this point. It translates that back into disc form. There are a variety of things that are occurring in that nature. We had a visit from a gentleman from the Library of Congress a few weeks ago, Dave Remington, who some of you might know, and he brought with him some absolutely remarkable examples of the state of the technology of scanning and of storing on optical disks and then of reproducing once again. One of them was an illuminated manuscript, a page from an absolutely beautiful and marvelous work. He projected on the screen for us an image which was of such detail and resolution that you were certain it had to be a very fine quality photograph of the original work. It wasn't that at all. It was the result of digital encoding following scanning, storage on digital

Question: "I'd like to ask Mr. Brown and Mr. McCoy to tell us about the possibility of sharing resources?" ROWLAND BROWN: "we had discussions with RLG staff and board members with respect to ways in which OCLC and **RLG** might collaborate, cooperate, etc. Frankly, one of the problems, which is no fault of either party (it is a set of circumstances). . .That is to point out that the economic and political issues separating these networks are far, far more significant than technological issues of linkage. . . .It needs to be done but it's going to take a lot of patience and probably a fair amount of stability on the part of both organizations because of the time it takes to do it.''

form, optical disk and reproduction. It looks very much like the entire surface of the material, every wrinkle and blemish and every mark has been picked up and lifted off and can be presented back to us again. It's a remarkable experience to see that kind of a product, to know that today's technology can produce it; not however at cost which would make it practical to put into production use today but we know that it will be brought into production use tomorrow.

Question: I'd like to ask Mr. Brown and Mr. McCoy to tell us about the possibility of sharing resources?

Brown: Ever since I came to OCLC, back several months before I officially was on the payroll, we had discussions with RLG staff and board members with respect to ways in which OCLC and RLG might collaborate, cooperate, etc. Frankly, one of the problems, which is no fault of either party (it is a set of circumstances) but RLG has gone through a series of changes in management, which makes an in-depth exploration of collaboration difficult. I had come to a point with Ed Shaw, over a series of discussions, where I thought we were rather close to some kind of an understanding. I then had a discussion with Pat Battin, who was the interim director, only to find that Ed's views on that were not reflective of Pat Battin's and possibly others and I have no idea what the present thoughts are. I think a number of people that have pointed out that OCLC and RLG are two different kinds of institutions, not only by governance but the members being served, the structure, the economics, etc. That difference, in and of itself, presents some of the problems in terms of how one collaborates and cooperates. In a way, it's like a private and a public corporation. They're both private, but I'm saying that they start from a different economic concept. We are market driven; they are primarily driven, not by transactions, but more by other forms of grants and membership fees, foundation support, and soforth. That is not to say either one is better or worse, it simply means that when you put the two together in some collaborative form, there are lots of problems, more than just linking. Linkage is always described as another way in which all these networks can get together. Henriette Avram did us all a favor a couple of years ago. None of us have taken her up on it. That is to point out that the economic and political issues separating these networks are far, far more significant than technological issues of linkage. We've never considered the issue of linkage to be particularly difficult, quite honestly, but we have foreseen the problems of how a group of research libraries operating one way can link ef-

RICHARD McCOY: "One thing that I can say is that Ed Shaw and Pat Battin and Dick McCoy do share a common interest in sharing the resources which we have in the RLIN data bases . . . There are economics costs to doing it, by the way, if we provided the entire data base to OCLC or they were to provide their entire data base to us in some way. We would each be mightily challenged by the cost of loading that information onto the system. There would be a lot of benefits in return. . . . We think we need to do the work now, not because there are strong economic issues that say that we should be linking our networks right now. . . it would be somewhat costly to do that and there might be better ways of sharing data for the moment.''

fectively with a system which is very much designed to serve their special needs and is structured entirely different from ours, to work with an organization that has, yes, 70 to 80 research libraries but also has some four thousand others from those smaller libraries to the larger ones. It needs to be done but it's going to take a lot of patience and probably a fair amount of stability on the part of both organizations because of the time it takes to do it.

McCoy: I was surprised at the first part of the response and I apologize for our transition. It was only about six months long and I hope that I'm going to be there for a good long time. One thing that I can say is that Ed Shaw and Pat Battin and Dick McCoy do share a common interest in sharing the resources which we have in the RLIN data bases, as do our institutions individually and as a part of the partnership. I could give you a number of examples and specific reasons why, but let me choose two. Let me use the State of Minnesota and the University of Minnesota Library as one example and let me use Princeton as another. I could have picked other members of our partnership. Minnesota is really two things; it's a library, it's a major research library in support of the work going on, on the campus of the University of Minnesota. But in addition to that, by state law or constitution, I believe, and by tradition, it is the hub of a networking of state libraries. Minnesota, therefore, is very anxious to participate with its peer institutions through RLG and does that and it happens to do its technical processing work in RLIN. It's equally interested in serving its role with the rest of the library community throughout the State of Minnesota. It is going to be doing that and may be doing it at the moment through tape loading membership in OCLC and we're very pleased that was possible. We would hope in time that there might be ways to do it in which each institution might not have to negotiate separately with an individual network to make this happen. What we would really like to see is a very general sharing of the data resources and it perhaps could be done more economically if we did not do it by an institution by institution basis. I mentioned another example and that is Princeton. I select Princeton because they do not have that same responsibility within a statewide network. But Princeton is a good example of a motivation that I think most of our research universities hold. They feel an obligation to the support of scholarship in general. Wherever they hold materials that they believe of high value, not just to persons doing work at their institution, but to scholars doing work wherever they may be in this country or elsewhere, they are anxious to share that information. As a result, this dictates many things which they do. For instance, in RECON (Retrospective Conversion Activity) the kind of decision which Princeton makes, it simply cannot think of going back and converting all of its holdings, given current approaches to doing that. They imagine it would cost something like fifty million dollars to do it and the length of time and such would make it impossible. But they're making choices which are based on special roles which they have in support of the scholarly community. If they have collections which they believe to be of very high value, they will put their RECON activities there and at the same time they are anxious to make that data available as widely as possible. So these are the kinds of motivations that exist and I think that we're interested in encouraging as much sharing as can be supported. There are economic costs to doing it, by the way, if we provided the entire data base to OCLC or they were to provide their entire data base to us in some way. We would each be mightily challenged by the cost of loading that information onto the system. There would be a lot of benefits in return. One of them, of course, would be simply in the form of hit rates. Another would be in the form that I described of having things more generally and widely available. One other comment on linkage between networks—I guess we think it is reasonably difficult and that it is essential that we be doing the work to develop the technology and the technical standards and also the library standards and information standards to make it possible to share more regularly. We think we need to do the work now, not because there are strong economic issues that say that we should be linking our networks right now—it would be somewhat costly to do that and there might be better ways of sharing data for the moment. Because it is essential that we know how to do that, both to prepare for a future when the economics of sharing between networks will be different and it's also essential to us if we really believe that distribution is going to happen. In the stages of distribution over the next several years, before we're able to shift the entire data base out on an optical disk, for instance, we need to have networks which are able to communicate and the work that we're doing now in the linked system and standard network interconnection project, we believe, is an absolutely essential base for being able to do that kind of interconnection that distribution requires.

Brown: Could I add a couple of points? On the linked system project, probably not widely known, the article that I referred to earlier in my talk states the contrary, but OCLC, at its' own expense, has, from the beginning, had a technical party present during the discussions and in the exploration both of the technical side and the authority side, so in effect we have participated; we simply haven't participated in an official sense because we are not receiving any funding and did not ask for funding from the Council on Library Resources to do that because at that point in time we felt that we wanted to have our options open in terms of what was being developed in the commercial field and there indeed are a number of activities going on in the commercial vendor field that we want to look at equally. But we did participate, we have monitored it, we certainly intend to cooperate in any way that's necessary. The other thing is that I think is lost sight of and probably in a way it's treated editorially and journalistically but a great deal of collaboration goes on between those research institutions that are part of OCLC and those that are a part of RLG. In fact, we have varied committees, not only of ARL but committees of OCLC that have members of both organizations looking for common activities. Also, I think it is fair to say that every research library in RLG has a dedicated line into that institution and has a terminal, at least one, so that in effect, RLG institutions have never not been communicated with and know what's on and have access to OCLC from the beginning. Most of them are now, or will be shortly, tapeloading so that at least their holdings will be available to OCLC members in general for purposes of resource sharing. That's an added cost to RLG members to do that and we're trying to structure it in such a way that it is subsidized at the lowest cost as possible. Also, some of the networks have sought and received LSCA funds to enable those tapes, particularly the archive tapes (those tapes that go back beyond the current cataloging) to fund those on behalf of the resource sharing within their network. There are all kinds of things that are going on, perhaps more behind the scenes than is generally publicized, towards coordination. I see that improving all the time.

Question: Since it was mentioned this afternoon, what is the current prediction on when OCLC expects subject access?

Brown: First of all, and I would guess that both RLG and ourselves both dealing with the problems of very, very large data base much of which is never accessed after its original entry and indeed after RLG and OCLC institutions get through putting in all their archive materials that will only swell so while we hope we may both keep issuing releases of that how big our data base is the fact is that

RICHARD McCOY: "I think the appropriate measure that we need to apply [for subject access] is, what is the cost of getting out the material in some alternative way if you do not have an extensive search capability?"

the big data base is more of a problem than an asset, in many ways. The question is that most interlibrary loan activities, most subject teaching, most activity is dealing with a relatively small portion, probably of either one of our data bases. We have to structure the data base in such a way that it makes economic sense to do that. Now we talked about a subset, a working set, but it will basically take some portion of our data base mount it, and experiment with several different searching protocols. Test it in some locations and then determine its' workability, its' cost-effectiveness, how it will be used on a larger basis. That's the start. I would hope that we would be in a position to do that the next calendar year.

McCoy: Can I follow up on that? We are in the same situation in the terms of dealing with the problems of very large data bases and we do need to create searching strategies which are cost-effective. I think the appropriate measure that we need to apply is, what is the cost of getting out the material in some alternative way if you do not have an extensive search capability? I think when we explore some of the manual methods that are necessary when one has, for instance, only partial information, you do not have complete titles, you do not have identifying information and wish to get at it. If you compare that with the capability of searching a machine-readable and heavily indexed data base, the alternative costs are very high. At that point, I think the kinds of decisions that our institutions have been making to opt toward the more extensive kind of search strategy and I think will continue to do that. Searches are relatively inexpensive, even with partial information. By that particular kind of measure, a typical search costs a dollar or something in that neighborhood and for the end user that's pretty reasonable service.

Question: Only one of the speakers mentioned it this morning but what I was interested in is obviously ILLINET has been in the cooperative reference business for some years now. From the three, SOLINET, NELINET, and INCOLSA, what do they think the decisions are, or why, or why not does a network have reference or not have reference?

Markuson: The question is why we weren't in cooperative reference. I think that you mean the facilitating of actual answering of reference questions as opposed to information retrieval services. Am I correct? One of the reasons that we have not gone into that is that within our State, we have multi-county cooperatives within areas of the State and that is the function that they provide. Therefore, if we provided that, we would certainly be duplicating that service. It's not that we couldn't do it, but the members have never come and said they would want to. I would hope, however, that our networks would look at technology that would facilitate sharing of reference skills. I like to think of a library network for reference structured in such a way, for example—I happen to be interested in dance—the New York Public Library has probably the best dance collection that anyone with an advanced question could send it there. Like large scale, highly specialized reference networks. I was very disappointed, for example, when the Library of Congress had their state library hotline network. Couldn't have cost very much, but they couldn't support it. I think we do have better technology now with electronic mail and maybe telephone networks. Reference is an expensive service that could be networked. I would be interested in us exploring the technology to facilitate much wider. Right now, it's on a local area.

Mockus: I'm not sure if I understand exactly your question. In our case, I think there are mechanisms in at least five of our six states for that kind of hierarchy already and those mechanisms preceded OCLC. So again, so as not to duplicate what is already available, we would offer access to the automated systems.

Grisham: To do good reference work, you've got to have an excellent collection and the networks do not have a collection and so it's a matter of putting into a major collection a resource person who could answer as a backup or respond to the reference work that's going on out in the libraries and that concept is at work. It's probably something that we could support and push as a concept but I don't see us, as regionals, having staff to do reference work to backup locals. We find it already working successfully in some other areas.

Kaser: At this point, I'm going to thank this magnificent panel for their presentations today and I'm sure you share that appreciation with me.

I want to express for the panel its' appreciation for the hospitable reception and the very kind attention and very vigorous discussion which you have contributed to this meeting as well.

As a last item, and I have been stopped from naming names in this regard, I'm sorry about that because I would like to do it. I think the planning and the logistics behind this whole Conference have been excellent. This, I understand, has been the work of the Lincoln Trails Library System and Eastern Illinois University and the University of Illinois at Urbana, but the individual psyches that participated in this show remains nameless but we're grateful to them anyway.

And now, let's have one of these every month. Thank you for coming.

THE SPEAKERS

Front Row: Laima Mockus, Executive Director, NELINET; Barbara Evans Markuson, Executive Director, INCOLSA; Toni Carbo Bearman, Executive Director, National Commission on Libraries and Information Science;

Back Row: Richard McCoy, President, RLG, Inc.; The Honorable Jim Edgar, Secretary of State and State Librarian of Illinois; Frank Grisham, Executive Director, SOLINET; David Kaser, Professor, School of Library and Information Science, Indiana University; Rowland Brown, President and Chief Executive Officer, OCLC, Inc.

For Product Safety Concerns and Information please contact our EU representative GPSR@taylorandfrancis.com
Taylor & Francis Verlag GmbH, Kaufingerstraße 24, 80331 München, Germany

www.ingramcontent.com/pod-product-compliance
Lightning Source LLC
Chambersburg PA
CBHW052130300426
44116CB00010B/1843